YOU'RE NEXT!

TURN YOUR DISAPPOINTMENT INTO DESTINY

ELAINE DURAN
with JULIE VOUDRIE

You're Next! Turn Your Disappointment into Destiny

Elaine Duran
Enticing Cake Boutique
www.enticingcakeboutique.com
info@EnticingCakeBoutique.com
Phone: 321-299-5483

ISBN-13: 978-1541153127

Printed in the United States of America

First Printing

Dedication

To my super hero, Grandpa Oscar

Only a heart as dear as yours would give so unselfishly. Thank you for being so transparent in your faith and expressing your love for the Father. For all the times you held my hand and called me your "doll". You took your precious time and invested in me. Your love, kindness, and generosity has left an imprint in my heart forever.

Our Appreciation to:

Elaine wishes to thank:

God, the lover of my soul. The One who puts these desires in my heart and continues to keep me and bless me. Light my path and lead the way because wherever You send me I will go.

David, the love of my life, my husband, my best friend, an amazing father to our two children. The one who makes me laugh, wipes my tears, and holds me tight; you've seen me succeed and you've seen me fail and have cheered me on with undeniable commitment.

My greatest joy, my miracle babies, Valentino and Natalia. God showed me favor and now my life is complete with you in it. You make my world a beautiful place.

Mom and Dad, I have no words to acknowledge the sacrifices you made and the dreams you had to let go just to raise me so I could have a chance at attaining my own. You did the best you could with what you were given; I am extremely grateful and love you both dearly.

To my biggest fan, my sister Jeannette, my one and only. Thank you for insisting I put in for *Next Great Baker*. I did it and there's more to come!

To Bishop Dr. Mark Chironna, my spiritual father. It's been an honor to be under your covering for so many years. The investment you've poured into my life has been richly received and valued. I appreciate you.

To my dear friend, Julie: who would have thought that our friendship would grow after meeting on a T.V. show and that a word spoken over my life would come to fruition because of your God-given talents? It has been an honor to call you my friend and I am so thankful for your incredibly sweet generosity. Thank you for believing in my story.

Julie wishes to thank:

My husband, Jeff, and the rest of my family, for encouraging, supporting, and believing in me throughout this project; Annie Hollingsworth, for editing; Elaine and David Duran, for allowing me into your home and hearts and trusting me to share your story; and last, but not least, Abba, my everything.

Table of Contents

Foreword

The first time I met Elaine and David Duran was at Carlo's Cake Factory in Hoboken, NJ. We were preparing for an adventure of a lifetime as contestants on TLC's *Next Great Baker* and I remember being impressed by this dynamic couple's warm, outgoing personality. As the days went by, they were a source of strength and encouragement to me on more than one occasion, but never more so than on my final day.

My daughter and I had been eliminated and it was time for us to return home. I managed to keep my emotions in check, until I faced some logistical issues with our packing. I couldn't hold back the tears anymore as my exhaustion, disappointment, shame, and frustration bubbled over.

While my daughter stood by watching her mom have a little meltdown, David and Elaine walked by and gave me a hug. I didn't realize until later that Elaine had slipped a wad of cash into my pocket, and her gift helped relieve one of my shipping issues. But even more meaningful was having that act of kindness in a difficult moment and the timely comfort that it brought.

Fast forward one and a half years later, to when the Duran family dropped by our home around Christmastime, as they were vacationing nearby. As we sat together catching up, Elaine shared her dream of writing a book one day.

"But I'm not a writer," she said.

I told her, "Well, I am!"

As she continued to share her vision of a book, the ideas and form flowed effortlessly in my mind. I grabbed a notebook and we began sketching out ideas. I realized that what she wanted to accomplish was not only possible, but that we could partner together to make it happen.

Four months later, I was sitting in Elaine's living room, video recording the story of her life. While I already knew a part of her history, I was amazed at her transparency and how she had overcome adversity time and time again. It was only then that I understood the full significance of Elaine's final act of kindness when I left the show.

That day when I was having my mini meltdown, I had no idea how tight their finances were. I had no idea that they were struggling to pay the bills. I didn't know they had managed to scrape together a little cash so they could go into New York City, find some souvenirs for their kids, and have a little fun for themselves. I had no way of knowing that when Elaine saw me standing there in distress, that she whispered to David, "She needs it more," and selflessly slipped the money out of her pocket and into mine.

Elaine's passion to bless others is not fake, insincere, or shallow. The lessons she presents in this book aren't just ideas to her; they are how she lives life, every day, in hard times and good times. Elaine has paid a very high price for the truth she so willingly shares in these pages. The privilege of laboring together to translate her precious life experience and wisdom into print has been an extreme honor for which I will be forever grateful.

Elaine didn't know that when she sowed a seed of kindness into my pocket that she would reap the realization of her book dream. That's just one lesson we can all glean from Elaine's life. And you'll discover many more as you read the pages to come. As my time on this project comes to an end, there's just one more thing I want to say:

Elaine, you may now officially call yourself a writer!

Blessings,

Julie Voudrie

PART ONE

1

INTRODUCING...
ELAINE DURAN!

The sound of applause filled the auditorium as the latest presenter left the podium. The Miami Culinary Institute's Chef Coat Ceremony was nearing its completion and only one speaker remained: me. With a pounding heart and sweating hands, I quickly rehearsed what I had planned to share with this crowd of young, hopeful chefs. I knew it would take more than my bright red chef coat from TLC's *Next Great Baker* to hold their attention and earn their respect. But all I had to share was my life story of how in five short years I'd gone from making my first decorated cake to competing on a nationally televised cake competition show. Would my story be good enough? My thoughts were quickly interrupted as the Chair of the Miami Culinary Institute, Chef Collen Engle, began my introduction.

"I'd like to introduce to you Elaine Duran, who has come all the way from Kissimmee tonight to speak to you. We first met her at the home show here in Miami. A cake decorating class led to a call from TLC and an offer to appear in *Next Great Baker's* fourth season where the Durans made over-the-top desserts and won the Carrabba's Dessert Challenge, placing their Duran's Divine Pineapple Cake in 240 of the chain's restaurants." Chef Engle went on to describe my cake business, Enticing Cake Boutique, and my future plans, as he welcomed me to the stage.

As the crowd applauded my entrance, I felt like I was having an out of body experience. Hearing myself introduced like that left me amazed at how far I'd come in such a short time. Was that really me he was describing? Had I actually done all those things? And would the story of my life journey inspire this graduating class of new chefs to boldly move into the next step of their own lives?

Who would have guessed years before, when I didn't know the difference between fondant and fondue, that I'd be standing on a stage like this, speaking to a room of skilled chefs? Or during those hard, hungry times, when I was barely surviving on cans of tuna and staggering from the biggest betrayal of my life, could I have imagined that a dessert I created would be served in a national restaurant chain? And what about when I was struggling in high school, when I thought no one cared about me or my graduating? If someone had told me that I'd be the keynote speaker at a respected culinary school's chef coat ceremony, would I have believed it?

No, of course not. Back then, I sure had my doubts. And there's a good chance that today, you have doubts about yourself: doubts about your future, your potential, or your worth. Maybe, just like I used to be, you feel trapped, forgotten, hopeless, and discouraged. Perhaps life hasn't turned out the way you planned, or you're afraid to step out into an uncertain future. You might have suffered a big loss or a big setback. There might be something inside you that screams to come out, but you can't find your voice. Whether it's unfulfilled dreams, delayed desires, or a lack of purpose or direction, there are times in life when we all feel like we're on the road to nowhere.

We feel stuck. Stuck in a dead-end job or a bad relationship. Stuck in poverty or stuck holding the bag. Stuck in the past or stuck in a rut. Stuck living under someone else's expectations and not following our own dream. Sometimes life throws us a curveball and we instantly know we're headed down the wrong road. Other times, many miles go by before we wake up and realize that something is wrong, something is missing.

You see others succeeding. But when will it be your turn? Have you been passed by? Passed over? Maybe the struggle and the fatigue are so great you're about to pass out. Is there any hope that you can have the life you've always wanted?

The answer is yes. 100%, absolutely, no-doubt-about-it yes. How can I be so sure? Because it happened to me. In Part One of this book, you're going to see my journey: the good, the bad, and the really bad. I'm not going to sugarcoat anything and I'm not going to hype it up, either. I'll tell you straight up like it was. Maybe there will be parts of my life you can relate to. But let me tell you, the struggle was real, and none of us make it through life without a few struggles along the way.

Was it easy to turn my disappointments into my destiny? Not by any means. It took a lot of guts, hard work, and more than a few false starts before I found myself on the right road at last. And yes, there were a few detours on the way, along with some major potholes and more than a few speed bumps.

In Part Two, I'm going to share with you all the life lessons I've learned on my journey. I want to help you uncover the way to your dreams so you can find your voice. I want you to discover the amazing person you are and gain the courage to start living out your own unique destiny. And I want to share the practical steps I took (and still take) to get turned around, get on track, and stay on track.

You're next. You can turn your disappointment into destiny. You don't have to settle for life as you've known it. There are steps you can take, today, to move closer to your dreams. That's the process I'm still in myself. This book isn't written by someone whose every dream has come true. While I've experienced a degree of success, I have even greater dreams I want to see fulfilled. I still have to make choices every day that either take me further away or closer to my goals. You and I are in this destiny struggle together.

My life story may not make a good script for a Hollywood movie, but it's real and it's all I've got. Will it be enough to hold your attention? I'm not really worried about earning your respect; I've learned to respect myself no matter what other people think. But my goal with this book is to prove one important point: If I could find a way to take my struggles, failures, and losses and turn them into a life filled with hope, joy, and purpose, anyone can; even you.

So let me introduce you to a little Puerto Rican chica and the path she took from the middle of nowhere to a national stage. And then we'll work together to help turn your disappointments into the destiny you've been waiting for. You're next!

2

THE BEGINNING

I was a 70's baby, born in Delaware. Along with my sister, who was one and a half years older than me, we had a good, innocent childhood. Though my parents were both Puerto Rican, I don't remember race being an issue, even though it seemed we were the only Hispanic family in our mostly white neighborhood. When you're young, you don't think about how many Hispanics and how many whites and how many blacks, until you're playing in the school yard and the kids call you "Indian" because of your black braids and darker skin.

Only a master stylist could have dealt with my curly, frizzy hair, so to tame the "beast," Mom would give me these cute braids that I just loved. When the kids called me "Indian," in essence, they were right, because the Puerto Rican culture is a mixture of Taíno Indian, African, and European White.

I would defend myself and say, "I'm not Indian, I'm Puerto Rican!" But it never felt racial to me. I just wanted them to know the truth about my heritage.

The truth about my parent's relationship wasn't as clear to me then as it is now. Mom worked various office jobs with a priority to put food on the table. Dad would help as much as he could, but his true passion was music and strumming his guitar. While Mom had the stronger work ethic, Dad was like a big teddy bear and was a caring and nurturing father, always loving on us. But his musician personality clashed with Mom's practical focus on financial security, creating tension that would grow over the years.

Even though Mom was very down-to-earth and a realist, she was very girly girl. My sister and I always loved that about her and we enjoyed watching her wake up in the morning and put on her makeup and perfume. She would look and smell like a million bucks. Mom would put her high heels on because she was five foot nothing and wanted a little more height, and she'd go out like she was going to conquer the world. But my sister and I weren't like that. It took us a little longer before we started to care about our appearance.

A Natural Born Optimist

One thing I did care about early on was winning. I was born an optimist and that became really obvious one day when I was around six years old and we went down to our local K-Mart. It was Easter time and they had an Easter coloring contest. The prize for the winner was this huge Easter basket and I said to myself, "Look how big that Easter basket is! I'm gonna win that Easter basket."

My sister and I each got the coloring page with a little chick and Easter eggs on it and as I colored my page, I said a little prayer. I had been faith taught from a young age so I said, "God, if you'll allow me, I'll color this, and I know that with You, I can win this." I colored that page with all the faith I had in my little itty bitty heart and turned in my entry.

This is where my optimist side bumped heads with my mom's realistic side, which sometimes bordered on pessimism. I just knew I was going to win that basket, but Mom said, "What if you don't?"

I couldn't stand to hear the word "if." That word was not an option for me. Even though Mom doubted my optimism, sure enough, a few days later we got the phone call that I had won the Easter basket. That was enough to set me up for a life of dreams.

Not long after, my fresh burst of optimism was put to the test. It was another coloring contest, but this time at school. They used a little bumble bee mascot to teach the kids the importance of buckling up. I can't even remember what the prize was, because at the time all I really cared about was proving that I could win. I had already won the Easter basket, so I knew I could win this contest, too.

Even as a young child, "no" was not acceptable for me. It wasn't my parents that taught me that; it was just how I was wired. My dad never imposed his ideas on me. He'd give me his opinions, but let me make up my own mind. My mother, on the other hand, always had something to say. But I understand now where she was coming from, because as a mother she was being a protector. She didn't want my feelings to get hurt if my dreams didn't come true.

My response at the time was, "What do you mean if I don't win? Of course, I'm gonna win."

And sure enough, just like the time before, I won the coloring contest. Of course, I knew I was going to win all along, even if Mom didn't believe me. This wouldn't be the last time I would hold on to see my dreams come true against some long odds.

Grandpa Oscar

While Delaware was where we lived, it wasn't the place we called home. Home was in Philadelphia, at Grandma's house. Out of respect, every Monday, Wednesday, and Saturday, we'd visit my mom's mother and that's where we got to enjoy our Puerto Rican culture. The only bad thing was that my grandparents lived in a really rough part of town, in a drug-infested ghetto. By the time I was eight years old, our family moved to Philly to be closer to our extended family, which included aunts, uncles, and cousins. But Mom made sure we lived in the suburbs where it was safer.

Once we moved to Philly, I got to spend more time with my favorite person in the world: Grandpa Oscar. I'd been told from the beginning that Oscar wasn't my "real" grandpa. There had been a tragic house fire when my mom was a little girl, and even though she and her four siblings survived, her father didn't.

Later, when the kids were still very young, Grandma, who was a short, dark Puerto Rican with large red lips and big fuzzy hair, fell in love with Oscar. A former military man, Oscar was a green-eyed, light-skinned Puerto Rican. Even though Grandma would point to a picture on the wall and tell us that was our "real" grandpa, Grandpa Oscar was the apple of our eye; no one could ever take his place.

I remember sitting next to him and spiking up his hair real high or watching him use his big muscles to carry a refrigerator on his back, up the stairs of an old Philly row house. He'd stand up and flex his biceps so my sister and I could hang from his arms like monkey bars.

Grandpa Oscar was our guardian angel. I remember Dad would chase after us, wanting to discipline us for something and Grandpa Oscar would get in the way and say, "You're not spanking her!" Other times he'd tie my loose tooth to a door knob then slam the door, and there would go my tooth, but it wouldn't even hurt.

One time he literally saved our lives. It was Halloween day and along with some cousins, we'd gone to play at a fenced-in empty lot Grandpa had next to his house. He'd given us a big refrigerator box to play in and the four of us were sitting like little sausages inside the box, making it rock back and forth.

But then we heard rattling on the chain fence and we heard some kids say, "Yeah, they're in there." We looked out of the box and saw a gang of three kids, all dressed in black, wearing Halloween masks and holding baseball bats. We didn't know it, but they'd been watching us for a while and when we went into the box, they thought we'd be an easy target.

When we saw them jumping the fence, we yelled out, "Grandpa! Grandpa!"

And he came running out of his house with a bat of his own, in full hero mode, with the gang of kids running for their lives.

He was the most amazing, loveable, inspiring entrepreneur I've ever met. He had a hardware store, helped start up a pizza place, and flipped homes in the heart of the ghetto, just to help people who couldn't afford housing.

He would take us to homes he wanted to buy, with holes in the stairs because they were so old, and tell us, "I'm going to buy these houses, and at the end of the day, it's all for you, my grandchildren, because I love you so much!"

Even though he lived very humbly, he was the go-to person in his neighborhood. He'd walk around with holes in his shirt so we called him the "Holy Man." He drove an old rattly car with a loud muffler so everyone knew that Oscar was coming down the street. He'd known real poverty as a kid and chose to live well below his means. But people on the street knew that he was the man with money even though he went around as if he had nothing to show for it. Every time he took his money out of his pocket, it was this big wad of cash. Maybe it was all ones, but as a kid it looked like a bundle to me.

People would come up to him and say, "Hey Oscar, I need $20 for something."

Or, "Oh, Oscar, we couldn't pay this bill and we need $500."

And he'd pull out that big wad of cash and help them out. It's almost as if all his investments were done just so he could turn around and bless people.

Grandpa Oscar taught me my first lessons about money. He told me, "If they ask you for money, and you have it, give it to them. If they come back and ask you again, give it to them again, because the reason you have it is so that you can bless someone else. But if they ask you for money and they promise to pay you back, hold them accountable. And if they don't pay you back, yet they ask you for more, tell them no, because they didn't keep their word as a man."

I saw him walk out this principle time after time. And people treated him like Robin Hood as a result.

I never saw him use his money on himself. It was always for others. One time I went into his basement and saw it filled with boxes. When I asked him why, he said, "Well, the Dominican Republic don't have Bibles, so we're shipping these boxes of Bibles out to them."

I'd see him counting out cash and he'd say, "I've got to go to the bank because I just sold something. But the Dominican Republic doesn't have a church in this one town, so we're going to go and build them one."

One day I saw him packing up luggage and I asked him where he was going. He told me, "We're going to the Holy Land. We want to get a little closer to God."

Whatever he did with his money, it was always centered on love, faith, and blessing others.

Through all these actions, Grandpa Oscar left a permanent imprint on my life. He taught me how to have authenticity and how to love - truly love - and not expect it back. He was incredible. And he continued to be an influence for good in my life for years to come. To this day, he has been the most amazing person I have ever met.

Ghetto Memories

While Grandpa Oscar gave me lots of great memories, the ghetto he and Grandma lived in left me with some pretty bad ones. One morning after I'd spent the night at my grandparent's house, I woke up and looked out the window of the row house they lived in and saw the outline of where a dead person had been on the sidewalk. Apparently, someone had died there overnight while I'd been sleeping. I remember walking the ghetto and seeing syringes lying around on the ground. Thankfully, I didn't play with them.

One thing that made my time in the ghetto a little different was the fact that some of my uncles were known on the streets. If I was out with my cousins, people knew whose kids they were so I would be safe, too. But that didn't stop one of my aunts from getting mugged right in front of me. And though it never happened, looking back, I can see that getting caught up as an innocent in a drive-by shooting was a real danger.

In the midst of this gritty reality, I was left untouched and I still felt protected. Part of it was childish innocence that didn't know any better, but there was something deeper that stayed with me through my life. I had a knowing that no matter how bad the situation, my destiny would not be denied. And the eternal optimist in me stayed strong.

Moving to Puerto Rico

By the time I was thirteen, my extended family and I moved from Philly to Puerto Rico. That's one thing about the Hispanic culture: family sticks together. If one goes, we all go. Even if you don't get along, you stay together and deal with the dysfunction. My mom was able to relocate with an office job at a boiler company in Ponce, P.R., and her excellent English was one reason why. But the biggest change for my sister and I wasn't the fact that we would be immersed in a Spanish speaking world. There was another reason: for the first time in my life, I felt out of place.

The American urban culture we were accustomed to in Philly was very different than the island culture we encountered in Puerto Rico. We were used to being very tomboyish, playing handball and tag on the streets, with fire hydrants being popped open to create our own waterpark. But the island culture is much more refined, where the women are very ladylike and the girls are very prissy, with their dainty bows and carefully maintained hairdos. God forbid that one of their perfect hairs should fall out of place.

On top of that, to help us not lose our language skills, my sister and I were enrolled in a private Baptist school that taught in English, which was like the island culture times one hundred.

I remember my first day of school there. They sat me down next to a girl and she said, "Great. They're going to sit the Americuchi next to me."

Apparently, that's what the kids called English speaking girls that moved to Puerto Rico. I was ready to take off my earrings, put on some Vaseline, beat up the chick and teach her a lesson she'd never forget. But I didn't. Remember, the word "no" was not an option for me. I determined then and there that this girl was going to like me, whether she liked it or not.

And over time, that's exactly what happened. I remembered something my Grandpa had taught me: you kill with kindness. Because she struggled with English, I was able to help her with her school work and eventually we became the best of friends.

She wasn't the only person I decided to set out to conquer. Now that I was a young teenager, I was beginning to like boys, but I still didn't care much about my looks. I was overweight and my mullet short hair looked so awful, people would come up to my mom and say, "Oh, your boy is so cute!"

And Mom would snap back, "She's not a boy, she's a girl!"

Mom would tell me, "You know, the boys aren't going to like you if you don't do your hair. You need to care about your situation."

My "situation" wasn't helped by the fact that I still had multiple dark scars on my face from a cooking accident that happened when I was twelve.

There was one boy I liked in particular and I remembered what Mom had said about caring about my looks. And while I hadn't done anything to improve my "situation," I decided to go up to the boy anyway, with absolutely no shame, and tell him in a sassy way, "I like you, and what are we going to do about it?"

My mom thought I was crazy when I told her what I had done, but I was so confident in myself that I knew I could win him over. He didn't share my enthusiasm, but he did agree to become friends. Maybe it was because he had a crush on my thinner and prettier sister. Regardless, the experience didn't put a damper on my self-confidence.

The "Beauty" Pageant

Because Puerto Rico is really into pageantry, modelling and etiquette, my mom signed up my sister and me for a beauty pageant, hoping to help us tomboys fit better into the island culture. Pageant scouts had approached my mom asking about my sister, but when they took one look at me, a chubby short girl with a scarred face and crazy afro-puff hair, they said they didn't want me.

Bless my mom, she put her foot down and said, "If you don't take both of them, you're not taking the older one."

I remember thinking to myself, "Why don't they want me? What are they missing?" Because of how I was wired for confidence, I said to myself, "Just put me in that pageant and I'll show you how I can win it."

After going through all the pageant training, the day of the competition finally arrived. While my sister had this lovely lavender gown that fit her so beautifully, I wore this poufy peach taffeta dress that couldn't hide my baby fat. But I felt so glamorous in that awful 80s gown, even when they gave me the number thirteen. Of course, our family and friends were there to see us.

When I stepped out on that stage, I forgot all about how they had trained us to pose gracefully and instead gave one of those fierce model poses that must have left my family shaking their heads in embarrassment. No one but me was surprised that I didn't win, but my sister won most photogenic. I was happy for my sister, but I thought,

"Are they missing something? Are you kidding me? Just look at how beautiful I am. Why didn't they pick me?" My eternal optimism remained intact.

In Over My Head

Another thing that stayed intact was the same feeling of protection I'd had in the Philly ghettos. Even though I would be in situations where I could have gotten hurt, nothing ever happened to me. One time I was at the beach and a big wave sucked me down and there was no floor beneath my feet. I was a horrible swimmer and I felt like I was drowning.

I shouted out in Spanish, "Help Me! Help!" while frantically waving my arms to get attention. At first my family just thought I was being funny, until one of my cousins realized I was in serious trouble. My soon-to-be brother-in-law swam out to help me, but the whirlpool current was too much for him.

He said, "Baby, I can't! I got to go!" and he had to leave me there.

On the inside I cried out, "Lord help me! I'm going to die!"

There were large rocks not far away and I knew if the waves pushed me that way I would be a goner for sure.

In desperation, I cried out one more time, "Help!" but this time in English. Besides my family, the beach was almost deserted. But I could see a white man with black hair and royal blue shorts who heard my screams. He ran across the beach and swam out into the water where I was fervently dogpaddling to try to stay afloat.

When he reached where I was he told me in English, "We're both going to drown if you don't push hard, because I can't make it out of here with you. So I'm going to push you as hard as I can, and you promise to swim for your life as far as you can!"

As he pushed me, he got sucked into the whirlpool himself and I didn't see him again until after I reached the shore. I was crying and he came up to me to make sure I was O.K. He disappeared and I never saw him again. But he saved my life. Nobody else was on the beach that day that could have helped me. It was like my guardian angel was looking over me.

One day that angel had to work overtime when I decided to walk down the street to visit one of my friends. After a few minutes, I noticed a blue truck slowly driving behind me and my Philly street smarts kicked in. I quickly realized no one else was near me on the sidewalk. My heartrate picked up along with my pace, but the truck stayed right behind me. Before long, the guy pulled up beside me. He called out through his open window, claiming my mom had phoned him from work and asked him to pick me up.

I knew this was a lie because mom was home cleaning the house. I asked him in a sassy way if that was true, what was the password? Mom and I had made this arrangement years ago when we lived in Philly to keep me safe, but I'd never had to use it before.

This ticked the guy off and I started running for my life. He stepped on the gas and turned right in front of me, slamming on his breaks and screeching the tires. He hopped out of the truck, threw open the passenger door and lurched toward me, demanding I get in.

Up the street I noticed a couple of men working on a car in their driveway and I screamed out, "Daddy! Help! This man is trying to get me!" Of course, I knew it wasn't my dad, but this creep trying to kidnap me didn't, and I needed assistance and fast.

These guys quickly figured out what was going on and rushed toward the man, wrenches in hand and ready to fight, just like my Grandpa Oscar had defended me years earlier. The man instantly jumped back into his truck and sped away, leaving me scared out of my mind, but thankfully, unharmed. I shudder to think what my story would have been like had things turned out differently.

My time in Puerto Rico was a time of personal transformation, inside and out. On the outside, my baby fat melted away as I finally blossomed into womanhood. My tomboy ways faded and while I still had mostly boys as friends, I wasn't afraid to show my feminine side. On the inside, I had fallen in love with my Spanish culture. And though I had been raised around people of faith, my faith became my own as I had a personal encounter with God that marked me for life. I would need to call on that faith many times in the years ahead.

On the Move Again

After three years of living in Puerto Rico, our extended family was on the move again and my mom found a job in Orlando, Florida. My sixteenth birthday celebration turned into a farewell party as my friends gathered to say goodbye. There were two significant moments I remember from this event. The first validated my ability to win no matter what. One of the guests was the boy I pursued early on. At the party, he confessed to me that over time, he developed a major crush on me but was too intimidated to let me know. And if only I was staying in Puerto Rico, we could have a relationship together. I had won the boy after all.

But there was another guest I had an eye on at the party. And he brought the biggest gift of all to make sure he stood out from the rest. We'd met six months before and instantly connected because we'd both grown up in the States. This was a relationship that would continue on, though at the time I had no idea how life-changing it would be. For now, it was simple puppy love. We promised to write letters and call each other, and I found myself wishing I didn't have to leave the island.

Once again, I had to change cultures. I felt just as out of place when I moved to Florida as I did when I moved to Puerto Rico. I didn't realize how much the island culture had changed me until I found myself finishing my junior year in an urban high school in Orlando filled with fighting, violence, and segregated races.

In Puerto Rico, it didn't matter if your skin reflected your European, African or Taíno heritage. All colors of skin could be found in the same family and everyone considered themselves Puerto Rican regardless. But now that I was back in the States, each race stuck together and wouldn't relate to the others. I didn't understand why it couldn't be one big happy place. I made a point to hang out a bit with each different group and found myself making friends across the different cultures.

Senior Year

For my senior year, the school district changed and I attended a more suburban high school. I immersed myself in the sport teams and other school activities, in part because I had learned to mix so well socially, but also to avoid the growing strife at home. Tension grew between my parents over financial pressures and personality differences, to the point that I wanted to stay away from it as much as possible. And because of this tension, in my teenage mind, I took it as rejection. I wanted them to be more involved in my life but it wasn't going to happen. And before long, even my beloved Grandpa Oscar disappointed me.

He had come to one of my soccer games. I wasn't playing soccer because I loved it; I was just trying to stay away from home. To be honest, I was horrible at soccer, but I really wanted my Grandpa to come and see me play anyway. When the game was over, I asked him if he enjoyed the game. Grandpa, who was a competitive go- getter, wasn't impressed with my play at all.

He told me, "You didn't win! What happened? You didn't even throw the ball the right direction!"

This was actually a major turning point in my young life. On top of what was happening at home, in my selfish teenage way of thinking, I made a conscious decision to not share my feelings with others anymore. Now it was me against the world. At the time, I didn't understand the pressures my parents and family were under. I just assumed that no one cared if I even existed; I wasn't important to them, so from then on I was going to live my life my way. And I went on to do just that.

A Royal Tantrum

I experimented with the party scene and quickly figured out that wasn't for me. My grades plummeted but I didn't care. I got D's and I was barely on track to graduate. But one thing I did care about was homecoming. I didn't just want to go; I wanted to be the homecoming queen. When I found out my dad's brother was getting married in Puerto Rico at the same time, I threw a major teenage tantrum when my mom tried to force me to attend the wedding. I didn't care about family anymore at this point. It was all about me and what I wanted.

I told her, "This is really important to me. I'm going to go to homecoming and I'm going to win. I don't want you to go to the wedding. I want you to be here and I want you to see me get crowned."

Of course, Mom didn't think I had a chance of winning. And she didn't want me, her baby girl, getting my feelings crushed if I didn't win, when I could be enjoying myself in Puerto Rico instead. But to her credit, she bought me the most beautiful homecoming gown to make up for the fact that she couldn't be there.

I stayed with my aunt while my dad's side of the family went to the wedding. On the day of homecoming, some people from school casually asked me what color roses I'd want if I won, and what color Corvette I would like to be driven around in. I told them yellow was my favorite color, and at that point I just knew I was going to win. It took me back to my early childhood when I had won contests before. Why wouldn't I win this time?

Homecoming arrived and the homecoming court was announced. And sure enough, when it was time to announce the queen, they called out my name. I was crying my eyes out as they crowned me and gave me my gorgeous bouquet of roses. They thought I was crying because I was happy, but it was the most miserable day of my life up to that point. Though my aunts and cousins were there to support me, the most important people in my life weren't.

I thought to myself, "How dare they not believe in me? I knew I'd win."

And at that moment, I wanted to have a royal tantrum, throw my roses to the ground, and run for the hills. I wanted to say, "Keep your crown! I didn't want it. I was just trying to prove that I could win it."

But I didn't throw my roses and run. When my mom called later that evening to see how homecoming had gone, I didn't even want to talk to her on the phone. From that point on, I hardened my heart against my family and disowned everybody. While I managed to graduate, the hole in my heart just got bigger and bigger. I entered young adulthood with a lot of baggage and no sense of clear direction.

3

YOUNG ADULTHOOD

I managed to graduate high school and entered into the party scene again. I just wanted to dance, feel free, and not have anyone tell me what I could and couldn't do. Despite this, I had zero tolerance for the drugs, drinking, and sex, and a part of me still loved God. Somehow, in the midst of my searching, those core values stayed intact. But I wanted to taste the "real" world. There were times I would go into clubs and feel like I was in hell itself, with people high and drunk and doing all sorts of things in the shadows. But just like I'd sensed in the ghettos, or when almost drowning in the ocean, I felt covered and protected. I didn't know what I was looking for, but I knew I hadn't found it yet.

The party scene got old pretty quickly and I was ready to get a little more serious about my future. I was considering college and my Grandpa Oscar didn't want me to have to struggle my way financially through school. He took me to a six-month nail academy so I could learn a skill that would help me earn better than minimum wage. But he made me promise that I wouldn't quit on my college dreams. I was able to start working in my aunt's beauty salon while I enrolled in a local community college, eventually settling on an art major.

Direction at Last

I was still living at home at the time and one day my mom got a flyer that said, "Join us for Jam Night!" The graphics were very cool and it looked like an ad for a new club. Then in very fine print I saw that it was actually a church setting. I was impressed that a church would go to that much trouble to make their event look like a club night, so I decided to check it out. The scene was very relaxed, the music was pumping, and there was none of the stuffiness you often found in a traditional church gathering. The music was current, but the lyrics were Christian. And for the first time in a long time, I felt like I found what I had been missing.

I became totally committed to both Jam Night and the church, and after three months, the pastor approached me about becoming a part of the leadership. I wondered to myself if he would still ask if he knew what I had just come out of, but this was something I really wanted and I had a sense of belonging there. My self-worth was blossoming. I took the opportunity very seriously and consumed the Bible and any other book I thought would help me be the best leader I could be. We decided to make every Friday Jam Night, and soon I was combining my art skills and contagious enthusiasm to drum up interest in this weekly event. Before long, the youth group outgrew the Sunday service.

Finding "Love"

Around the same time, another major change happened in my life. My long-distance boyfriend I'd met in Puerto Rico moved to Orlando so he could go to college and we could take our relationship to the next level. But because he had to be a state resident for one year before he could qualify for financial aid, he had to put off college and get a job instead. As we got to know each other face to face, he joined me in my work at the church, mainly so he could be closer to me. As our courtship continued, he was very respectful of me and my family, and eventually he asked my father for my hand in marriage.

Not even 24 hours went by after we said "I do" before I knew something was very wrong. Though I had preserved myself for marriage, my husband wouldn't even consummate our relationship on our wedding night. I soon realized that I didn't know him as well as I thought I had, and his dysfunctional past became a part of our present life together. Communication was difficult and he would shut down whenever we needed to discuss anything. I was still young and naive and I did my best to be the little homemaker and be supportive of him, even when he asked me to quit college so I could spend more time at home.

Not long after I left home to get married, my parents' own marriage came to an end. Their differences in personalities and priorities became too much and there was nothing left to keep them together. While I was sad to see them divorce, I hoped that they would be able to find a better life apart.

I was still very active at my church and powerful things were going on there. Jam Night was getting bigger and bigger, and our prison ministry was having huge results as men's lives were being radically changed. While my husband joined me in these activities, I was the one who was in the forefront and I began to sense that he was both resentful and intimidated by our church journey. I struggled to keep in the flow of what was happening and be a "good" wife at the same time. But amazing things were going on and I knew it wasn't because I was so special. I was just thankful to get to be a part of it.

Pete

One story from this exciting time stands out to me. With my faith on fire like never before, I was looking for opportunities to make a difference in people's lives. I was working at my aunt's beauty salon in a low-income area doing nails and people would come in off the street all the time selling things. I didn't realize at first these were stolen goods, but everybody loved buying these name-brand items at rock bottom prices.

One guy in particular kept coming around. His name was Pete and he was a drug addict. He'd bring in genuine Polo shirts with the price tags on them, and I was so dumb and naive I didn't question where they'd come from. I was just impressed that they were obviously legit.

One day, Pete came into the salon with more stuff to sell and he looked like he had just gotten his fix. And it finally hit me: He was stealing this stuff and I was helping sustain his habit by buying it. I started crying because I felt so guilty.

He came over to where I was sitting and said, "What's up, baby? I got some more stuff."

I asked him to show me what he had, but I was really trying to set him up. As tempting as it was to buy what he had, I told him, "Pete, I can't buy from you anymore, because I am just as guilty as the person who first introduced you to your drugs. I love you that much that I can't buy this anymore. I've come to love you for Pete, not for the stuff you bring."

I told him that I didn't have any money to give him, but I would give him my friendship and he could come in and visit me anytime he wanted.

Pete was touched by what I shared and he told me no one had ever said anything like that to him before. Then he shared his life story.

He said, "I used to be pastor, but I couldn't take the process and the stress. So I started shooting up. And I lost my family and I lost my kids. If you hadn't shared what you did, it never would have caught my attention. I don't want to live like this anymore."

I was so fearless in my faith, I had him come to the back of the salon with me to take advantage of his desire to change. He broke his syringes and handed them to me. My husband and I took him to a local shelter, but they wouldn't have any space until the next day. We gave him just enough money to get a bus ride back to the shelter the following morning, but we never saw Pete again.

While I was heartbroken that I never saw Pete get free, there were plenty of others I did see reach that place. But the success and explosive growth of the youth and prison ministries made the church uncomfortable and my husband had to face his own internal issues as others around him were finding freedom.

Finally, it all came to a head and we made the difficult choice to leave that church and those ministries behind. We began attending Bishop Dr. Mark Chironna's church. Over and over again, leaders both in and out of the church, who didn't even know each other, would speak the same, powerful words over our lives about our destiny. The promises were so encouraging and just fed my hunger for more.

From Bad to Worse

But instead of making my marriage better, things only got worse. What I didn't know at the time was that my husband was leading a secret life. He was being unfaithful and had all sorts of hidden agendas. Even a family member saw him out with the "other" woman.

A guest speaker at our church, who, like me, didn't know what was going on behind the scenes, spoke over us that our marriage was about to be severely tested and encouraged us to pass the test. The handwriting was on the wall, but I didn't know then that in just a few short months, my husband would drop the biggest bombshell of my life.

It was the week of my birthday and my husband sat me down face to face, and for the first time ever, shared his true feelings with me.

He said, "I want out. I can't handle the process. I can't commit to this relationship anymore. I don't want to keep anything. You can have it all: the house, the car. I'm so desperate I just want out. I love you, but I'm not in love with you and I will not take another day. I'm out, today."

And he got up and left. He ran from our home and he ran from our marriage.

I was in total shock. I couldn't believe what I was hearing. How could this be happening to us, to me? How could he have hurt me so deeply? I had been faithful to him, sacrificed for him, and loved him with all my heart. I didn't deserve this!

It wasn't just my relationship with him, but our future together that was falling apart. I not only felt betrayed because he was unfaithful with the "other" woman, but also because he was unfaithful to our calling. All those words and promises were given to us as a couple.

I questioned God, saying "Now that he's not around, what's going to happen to the word you gave us over and over again? Does it all just go to crap?"

I was hurt, crushed and devastated.

I called my church right away and loving, qualified people were very discreet and offered professional counseling, therapy, and encouragement to help us through this crisis. Now that the mask was off, my husband's behavior became very irrational. My husband received separate therapy because he had so many wounds from his dysfunctional childhood. But after a while, the staff that had been working with him gave me a harsh bit of reality.

They told me, "Look. You're young and you have your whole life ahead of you. We've done the therapy with him but he isn't budging. He's not interested, and he doesn't even show up anymore. We have to tell you from a professional standpoint that you need to move on with your life."

I didn't want to hear this, but I needed to. For the first time in my life, a man failed me. Because I'd had such a loving father and grandfather, I was able to pick up the pieces and move forward. But this proved very hard to do. We had a brand new four-bedroom house and a brand-new car, with the payments to match. But I was determined to keep it all and prove to my soon-to-be ex that he couldn't ruin my life. And I wanted to prove to myself, my family, and the world that I could do it on my own.

The Starving Season

I needed to find a job and fast. Before the divorce was finalized, one of the jobs I got was at a wholesale wheel shop. The boss quickly figured out my situation and gave me a raise I didn't deserve. I also worked part time as a manicurist and at a department store, plus I sold silver jewelry out of the backseat of my car. I had to cut all my expenses to the bone, including my food bill.

But then I had another surprise. A 15-year-old cousin of mine wasn't getting along well with her family at home and she needed a place to stay. I couldn't leave her on the street, so I took her in. Together, we faked how lean our situation really was. Tuna fish became our staple and we'd split a can a day. My boss at the wheel shop began ordering big sandwiches for lunch, claiming he was too full to eat the rest, and then gave me half, which I'd take home and share with my cousin.

Looking back now, I find it hard to believe that she chose to live in such dire circumstances with me. Well into the night, she would sit and sleep for hours in my car, waiting for me to get out of my second job so we could both go home. She was in the middle of puberty and I couldn't provide enough food to sustain her developing body. All I could give her was shelter and my love. And even that was hard because I was so emotionally depleted. When she turned 16, she started working and brought home her paycheck to help out. We were just surviving together.

The struggle was real. For someone who had never experienced true hunger or abandonment before, it was a bitter pill to swallow. It felt like forever. For over six months I hid my desperate situation from my family. They didn't know I was sharing cans of tuna fish. They didn't know I was working four jobs to try to make ends meet. They didn't know I couldn't afford a decent meal.

At first, people would come up to me and say, "Wow, you look amazing! You've lost so much weight!"

But then later they'd say, "Oh my gosh, you're getting so skinny!"

They didn't know I was hungry and slowly starving because all my money went for bills.

Eventually, I was able to land a full-time job at the local sheriff's office and rent out the other bedrooms in my house to help keep up with the mortgage. I kept selling the jewelry as well, but at least now life was bearable. I was slowly picking up the pieces and moving forward. My dad, who had received some money through his own divorce, blessed me with it instead, which also helped me get back on my feet financially. My situation still wasn't great, but it was finally better.

The Man-Hatin' Season

The starving season was coming to an end but the man-hatin' season was in full swing! Because I was the "single chick," lots of guys thought they needed to get to know me or date me...even the married ones. But I was bitter at men.

I'm so glad I kept my morals and self-respect through this vulnerable period. I'd get so disgusted with married men who wanted a little sidekick relationship. In truth, the more they revealed their true colors of how easily they would be unfaithful to their wives, the more pathetic they appeared.

I developed a strong set of close friends to hang out with and I maintained an active date life, but I didn't have any serious romantic relationships. Coming from the beauty industry, I always kept myself put together and I remained fit, so guys were always hitting on me. But I continued to keep men at arm's length as most of them were only looking for what they could take from me.

During this season of my life, I just focused on how many hours I could work, how much jewelry I could sell, how lean

I could keep my expenses, and having a good time with my friends. I was in no hurry to get involved in a long-term relationship.

4

NEW BEGINNINGS

My 26th Birthday

My mom, however, had other ideas for my life. I think she was worried that her daughter would never find true love again. For my 26th birthday, some of my friends wanted to take me out to celebrate, so they got VIP tickets to go to a certain club later that night. Even my roommates were invited, so it was like a large entourage would be going. I really wasn't in the mood for a big party and I still wasn't sure I even wanted to go. But before that, I was going out to dinner with my whole family. Over the meal, Mom asked me what I was going to do later.

I told her, "My friends want to take me out, but I just want to stay in. I have to work tomorrow and I don't want to go anywhere."

But Mom said, "It's your birthday! You go out!"

I told her I really didn't want to, but she put her foot down. I guess Mom didn't want me to be single forever, especially when I saw the message she'd written earlier that day in the birthday card she gave me.

She'd written, "I hope you find the man of your dreams!"

I thought, "Why are you trying to marry me off and get me shackled down with some dude again? What's so bad about being single?"

Singleness had become a part of my identity. I struggled so much with my identity during this time, I even wanted to change my first name to something else. It was like I wanted a clean slate and a fresh start at life.

I knew I hadn't been named with intent by my mother. When I was born, she didn't know what to name me, so she took the suggestion of one of the nurses. I thought about the name change for quite a while and almost did it, but never followed through.

Now I'm so glad I didn't, for two reasons. One, because I later found out that Elaine means "shining light," so maybe there really was some divine intent when my name was picked out after all. The second reason is that in Spanish, my name is Elena, which is what my mother-in-law calls me all the time, so it's become a term of endearment.

Meeting "Raul"

But I wasn't feeling the love that evening. I was mad at Mom for putting that note in my card, but in the end, I reluctantly agreed to go. I got all dolled up and when my friends and I got to the club, I looked in to see what the club scene that night was like. The bouncer at the door asked for my I.D. and I gave it to him while I was still talking with my friends.

I didn't really notice he was there until I heard him say, "Happy Birthday." I thought that was such a nice gesture and I looked up to see a very attractive man with "Raul" on his name tag.

"Well, thank you!" I said, taking in how handsome he really was. But the very next thought that came through my head was, "He works here? At a club? No way."

On the inside I said, "Darn, 'cause he's a hottie," but on the outside I said, "Can I have my I.D. back now, please?"

But "Raul" said no. He was being a little feisty, which got my attention.

"What do you mean, 'No'?" I responded.

Now I was taking it a little bit personally.

"Why not?" I demanded again.

He said with a smile, "Because I like you."

I liked his assertiveness and his good looks, but everything else about him...well, let's just say I wasn't having it. He obviously wanted my phone number and was holding my I.D. as ransom. But I just wanted to get on with my evening and deal with him later. Besides, with all my friends in attendance, I'd have no problem getting my I.D. back.

Throughout the evening, "Raul" kept finding reasons to keep coming around where I was and while I felt some attraction, I mostly ignored him.

When we were leaving, I told him, "Hey, we've got to go. Can I please have my I.D.?"

His response was, "Only if you give me your number."

He went about it in a sweet, approachable way, and I knew I would never call him, so I decided to just give him what he asked for so I could get my I.D. and go home. There was no way I was going to get hooked up with a guy working at a club after all the hard work I'd gone through to get back on my feet!

As we exchanged numbers, I replied cordially, "It was nice to meet you, Raul."

He got a confused look on his face and said, "Raul?" And then he looked down at his name tag and explained, "Oh no, that's not my name. I forgot my name tag today. My name is David."

At that point, something shifted for me. Knowing about names and Biblical terms, the name "David" had great significance. The light bulb went off in my head.

"He's a leader," I thought to myself. "He's destined for royalty."

So then I started entertaining the thought that maybe, just maybe, I'd give him a chance, just based on his name. His name saved him, because "Raul" wasn't cutting it.

The next day I was back to work, going through my daily grind. A day went by and no phone call from David.

"See? I knew he wouldn't call. Why did I even waste my time with him?" I thought to myself. I was still man-hatin' but trying to let it go.

The second day went by, still no phone call. Mind you, I was used to well-to-do men catering to me. Here was this low-budget dude who had the gall to hold my I.D. just to get my number, and he wouldn't even call me? I was pissed.

Third day came, and again, no phone call. Remember, this was back in the day when beepers were around, before we had legitimate working cell phones. I was waiting on my landline to ring and it still wasn't happening. Before the third day was over, I said to myself, "The nerve of this guy! I'm going to call him and give him a piece of my mind."

I dialed him up and waited for him to answer, ready to rip him a new one.

"Hello?" I heard a male voice say.

Remember, there was no caller ID yet.

"Can I speak to David?"

"Who's this?"

"It's Elaine."

I was getting more ticked off by the second. There was a bit of a pause. I couldn't believe the nerve of this guy!

I shot back, "You remember? We met at the club?"

"I'm going to be really honest with you," he meekly responded. "I kid you not, I was just about to call you when the phone rang."

At this point, I thought he was full of crap and just trying to dig himself out of a hole.

"I had the paper with the phone number on it from the girl at the club, but I hadn't opened it up so I didn't know your name when you called. All I know was that I had to call you, but I've been working overtime and I was trying to be polite and follow the three-day rule, and today I finally had time to call. I knew I had to call today, because I didn't want you to think I wasn't interested."

Well, it was a little late for that!

Meeting David

He went on to say how much he'd been thinking about me and that he really wanted to see me. I agreed and gave him my address, but I wasn't excited about it. He had recently moved here from New York and didn't know the area very well. (GPS wasn't around then, either.) I got a phone call a while later, because he couldn't find my house. He was calling from the 7-11 around the corner and asked if I could just meet him there.

My expectations weren't very high, but they were about to get even lower. I drove up to the 7-11 and waited a few minutes for him to show up. But I didn't see him. I wondered if he was lost again, and then an old blue van I'd noticed when I first drove up caught my eye.

When the door opened on that van, the man I saw was not who I expected. Here I was, giving this guy the benefit of the doubt in not calling me in the first place and now he shows up in this crazy-looking van that makes him look like a stalker in a getaway car. I didn't even want to get out of my vehicle. I was totally judging him. I was used to a much higher caliber of success in my dates.

Mom had always told me to not a judge a book by its cover. But the first time I married, it was for purely for love. If I was ever to get married again, I planned to add success and financial security to the list. I was still young and naive, but I had experienced so much pain in my first relationship and I didn't want to repeat any of those mistakes.

What I found out later was that David was in his own hungry season. He had a past filled with baggage and his own drama with which he was struggling. He worked three jobs and had to ride a bicycle to work because his car was not drivable. He'd borrowed his dad's van so at least he could impress me with something because he didn't want to show up on his bike.

While his past was far from perfect, he was trying to make a fresh start and make something of himself. But I didn't know any of that when I saw him in the 7-11 parking lot.

I almost panicked. *How am I going to get out of this*, I wondered? I didn't want to take him home. In my mind, I felt like it was my life and I could choose who I dated. I was being so judgmental but I couldn't see that. I didn't know what to do.

He greeted me with his warm smile and while I wished for the earth to just swallow me up, I made a choice. Just like I had always done, I wanted to befriend the ones that were least liked. I decided to make him a friend. I would enjoy the evening, I would be cordial and be nice, but it wouldn't go beyond that. I could fake my way through it and not hurt his feelings.

He followed me to my house and my roommates were not impressed with him, either. They asked me later if I was desperate or something. But David was broken. We were all seeing that, but not the amazing man he truly was underneath. Over time, as I became David's friend and he became mine, that stellar character began to shine through.

David opened up to me right away and didn't want to hide anything, which was quite a change from my ex. I found out that evening that David was a supervisor for an airline company and he'd been living here with his parents for one year. He'd had a side gig in New York as a bouncer, which paid very well. While living in Orlando, he decided to be a bouncer again to have a social life and get acquainted with the area. He was trying to fix his car, as his had broken down on the move down to Florida. He talked about his personality, being a hard worker, and how he had to ride a bicycle to work.

For me, it spoke volumes. I sure wasn't rich, but I'd gotten to where I was because I busted my rear end and refused to give up. I saw that same fight in David. He understood the hustle. He might not be rich today, but the potential for success was in him. One difference between us was that I had refused to let go of my life when circumstances tried to tear it from me. David was out to create a good life for the first time.

David went on to share his personal side, telling how he'd grown up and the difficulties he'd had in his life. For example, when he was 16, his best friend got shot and died right in front of him, and something had stopped him from taking revenge and killing the suspect when he had a chance.

As he shared more stories from his past, it became clear to me that despite all the trauma and tragedy he'd experienced, the man I saw before me was destined for greatness. I told him I saw so much potential in him and that I didn't think he realized just how much potential he really had. Right from the first day, I began pouring life into him, like a thirsty plant in need of a good watering.

Love at First Sight...Not!

David knew from that moment he had found the woman of his dreams, but I still wasn't sure I had found the man of mine. The wish on my mom's birthday card would have to wait as over time David and I developed a good friendship together. Of course, he saw it as much more than that and quit his bouncer job right away. He didn't see the need to continue to look for a social life when he'd found the one he'd been searching for. For me, I enjoyed our growing friendship. We just seemed to click and within a short time, we were inseparable.

After being friends for several months, he could clearly see my financial struggle. The roommates in my house were starting to move out, creating pressure on my mortgage payment. I started working more hours between my four jobs at the sheriff's office, the department store, doing nails, and selling the jewelry, but it wasn't enough. David told me to stop selling the jewelry and let him do it instead. At least that way I'd only have three jobs instead of four.

Before long, David's coworkers at the airport were sporting silver jewelry. He even had them on payment plans and he would always remind them to pay up on pay day. His integrity and selflessness were so impressive.

"Who does that?" I thought. He wasn't even keeping a cut for himself.

While I appreciated all his hard work, with my roommates all gone, it still wasn't enough to make ends meet. Then David made me another offer.

He said, "Why don't you just take my paycheck from the airline? I don't need it. I'm still living at home, so I don't have all the bills. I'm saving my money so I can get my own place, but if you need it more than I do, I don't mind sacrificing until you can get back on your feet."

My Grandpa Oscar had taught me, "It's not how much money a man has, but how much he's willing to give you. If he'll give you all his $7 per hour, then you've got yourself a rich man. Because there are men who make $50 an hour, but don't want to give you a dime. But if he's willing to give you his whole heart and all his money? Then that man is a keeper."

I had always remembered that, and it was just this quality I was seeing in David.

I told him, "You're a keeper," and I meant it.

He began bringing me his checks, but I felt so bad taking them. I took his money out of desperation and out of pride, because I didn't want to tell my family my financial situation. But I knew something had to change. My solution was to ask him to at least be my roommate, since he was helping keep a roof over my head. He respected me and never asked to move in, but to be honest, I was falling in love with him – the real him – not some image or shallow exterior, but the real man on the inside.

Moving in and a Bump in the Road

Once he moved in with me, David's appearance began to change for the better. He enjoyed my cooking for him and gained healthy weight and color as a result. It was like his system was detoxing. But this was just the beginning.

After my divorce and before David came along, I had done some serious thinking about the kind of man I would want in my life. I realized that going the "religious" route didn't automatically result in faithfulness, so next time I would try something else. I made a list of what I would be looking for: a man who loved me for me, a good provider, and of course, faithful. But there was one thing I didn't exclude from my list: a man with addictions. I knew David was a smoker and that didn't seem like a big deal. But it took a while before I realized that David was an alcoholic.

Now that we were living together, I began to see certain patterns in David's behavior. He was so busy working during the week, he didn't have time to drink. But on the weekends, he bought several six packs of beer and, I realized, he chugged them all. I wasn't a drinker myself, and I figured he was just giving himself a break after a hard work week. Now I was noticing his hard drinking because he was spending more of his weekend time with me instead of with his family like he had before.

His bingeing behavior made him awkward, loud, and belligerent. Sometimes he would cry and ask me, "Am I a good person?" He was so drunk he wouldn't remember my answer anyway, and I realized that he was hurting down deep inside with feelings of shame. I was wondering if this was the drunk life and how I was going to handle it.

When I would try to get him to stop drinking after he had already started, he would get angry at me. I learned to wait until he was sober before we talked about it. When I asked him if he knew he had a problem with drinking, he completely denied it. He said it was just his way of blowing off some steam and it wasn't a big deal. I bought into it for a while because I'd never been around an alcoholic before. But his drinking problem didn't go away.

Now that he knew I didn't like it and he didn't want to lose me, he began hiding his drinking from me. I'd find bottles hidden around the house and in the car trunk. We'd been together six months by this time and this issue simply wasn't going away.

It all came to head that Thanksgiving. I had to pull a holiday shift at the sheriff's office and he asked to borrow my car so he could drive to his parent's house. He said he would come pick me up at 6 a.m. the next day when I got off from work. I knew that whenever he visited his family, he often got drunk.

I told him, "Sure, it's Thanksgiving, so go spend time with them. But make sure you don't drink because you've got to be sober so you can pick me up."

He said that would be fine, no problem. I thought he could handle it and so did he. We were both wrong.

After working a while, my supervisor told me I could get off work early. Then David gave me a call.

I told him, "Listen, they told me I could get out soon, so if you're even thinking of drinking and you're not even drunk yet, you need to come pick me up right now."

He sounded a little weird on the phone, but I had no idea he was already plastered. I didn't want to deal with this situation anymore and I was trying to get him home before he got drunk. But it was too late. I didn't want anyone else to know I was dating an alcoholic, so I was trying to hide it. That strategy was about to backfire, bigtime.

As I was waiting on David to come get me, a call came in. It was the Florida Highway Patrol.

"We've got a drunk driver in your county and we have to bring him in for an arrest. However, he says he has a girlfriend who works for the sheriff's office."

In my gut, I knew it was me. I was so embarrassed and I didn't want to say anything to the FHP officer. I asked him if I could call him back on a personal line and he agreed.

I called him back and said, "Hey look, it's me. I told him to come pick me up, so it's my fault he's on the road. It's not my fault he's drunk, and he should have told me, but I forced him to come get me."

The officer said, "I'm sorry, but I've got to arrest him. But I don't want to tow your car, especially if you need it to get to work tomorrow. If I leave it on the side of the road can you come get it before a tow truck does?"

I quickly called a good friend and said, "Girl, please. I know you're all the way on the other side of town, but can you please come and pick me up before they tow my car? If they tow my car, how am I going to get to work? This thing is going to get even uglier than it is. That man can rot in jail for all I care. I've been telling him to stop drinking, but this is it. As of this moment, it's over. I'm out of this relationship."

She said, "No problem. I'm leaving work right now and I'm coming to get you."

She came all the way to where I was to pick me up - an hour drive - then drove halfway back, so we could pick up my car. What a friend!

David was arrested, put in jail, and I left him there. I was so mad at him.

"Rot in jail! That's what you get. Now get sober." That's what I was thinking. I was done with him.

None of David's close family members were in town to come bail him out, either. I did my research and called the jail, but I didn't try to talk to him. I found out his bail was $500 and I knew he needed to learn a lesson, so I sure wasn't going to pay it.

Later he called me collect from the jail and I said, "It's over. I want nothing to do with you."

I was heartbroken. I thought he could change for me, but he hadn't. I realized I couldn't change him. Who was I kidding? He had to make that choice for himself.

He responded, "I'm getting out, and I'm not going to lose you. I'm going to fix this. I'm going to make it work. I just need help to change."

I wasn't convinced. I'd spent enough time at the sheriff's office that I'd heard this type of talk before and though maybe sincere at the time, people rarely followed through. But I was still in love with David, despite all the drama. I left him in jail for a few days, until he saw the judge and was released.

Of course, David said over and over, "I'm sorry. I'm going to change," but I didn't really want to hear it.

Time for a Change

Months passed by and it was apparent that David was desperate for change based on his ongoing effort. But there was something still missing in his life. One Sunday, David was up early getting dressed. I assumed he was going to visit his mother when he mentioned he was going to church with me instead. I knew that was one place David didn't want to be. He'd gone with me once before and then told me in no uncertain terms to never ever take him there again.

I called my mom to see if she'd like to go with us and we picked her up on the way. He seemed very happy that day and I couldn't believe it. Maybe jail had been his rock bottom after all. I went to church with a sense of expectation to see what God had up His sleeve.

We sat in the very back of the sanctuary so David wouldn't feel as out of place. At the end of the service, with every head bowed, there was an altar call where people could pray to ask God into their lives. David raised his hand, but I didn't see him do it. The Bishop said that for those who had prayed the prayer, he'd like for them to come on down so he could shake their hand. Without any hesitation, David stood up, boldly walked down to the front, and shook the Bishop's hand. He was the only one to do so.

David's life began a radical transformation from that point, but he knew he couldn't do it alone. He asked for help and he meant it. As we attended AA classes together, I became educated on alcoholism, and he went through therapy at our church. But the process took time.

He was able to quit the smoking very quickly, but the alcohol took longer to let go. He'd go sober for a few months and then he'd slip. Then he'd be sober for six months before he fell on his face again. Each time he'd feel like a failure and be so remorseful, but I'd encourage him that it wasn't the end of world, to pick up the pieces and get back up. Over time, he stayed sober and the cycle was broken. Amen!

5

NEW LIFE, NEW STRIFE

Months had passed. David was totally committed to his healing process and so was I. However, there was one thing that needed to change: we weren't married and I knew shacking up or living together was totally against what I believed in. I had a great respect for "the man upstairs" and I knew I needed to get serious about making the right choices.

I didn't know if David had marriage in mind at this point. Our life together had become a little too comfortable, but I kept waving my hand at him, doing the Beyoncé dance, singing, "You better put a ring on it." I told him if I was good enough to live with, then I was good enough to marry. Not too long after, at a family gathering on New Year's Eve, my soulmate knelt on one knee and popped the question. Of course, I said yes.

We looked forward to our married life together, but after David's long process of healing, it turned out I needed a little healing of my own. I realized I had fertility issues and having a family together was very important to both of us. I went to a specialist and tried different fertility drugs, but all I had to show for it was three miscarriages.

I was so discouraged, I even told David that it would be better for us to end our relationship, because I couldn't live with his regret of not being able to father his own children. David rejected that idea completely and said that he wasn't going anywhere and we could always adopt.

Eventually I did get pregnant - on our honeymoon, no less. But it didn't take long to realize something wasn't right. It turned out that I had an ectopic pregnancy and I lost one of my fallopian tubes. My doctor told me that now my chances of ever getting pregnant were very slim indeed. And all the stress I was under because I still worked several jobs wasn't helping my body get and stay pregnant.

I left the 911 dispatch job at the sheriff's office, but still held on to my nail job so I could keep my license current. And we needed the money. David and I had moved into a new house to go along with our new marriage and the mortgage wasn't going to go away just because I needed to cut my stress level.

Job of a Lifetime

One of my coworkers at the nail salon told me about an amazing new sales job she had with a telecom company and the big paychecks she was making. (When you have a nail license, you like to keep it active, even if you have a great job somewhere else.) I didn't believe her, and she promised to show me her next pay stub. Sure enough, when she showed it to me, she'd earned $6,000 for only two weeks of work. I was stunned and instantly asked for her boss's phone number. There was no way I could pass up this opportunity.

I arranged for an interview with her boss right away and touted all my sales experience over the years in the beauty industry. I told him if he would give me three months of his time I could show him what I could do. He was impressed with my go-getter attitude and offered me a job on the spot.

I was reinventing myself yet again as I bought corporate clothes and got dressed for success. I started the following Monday and hit it hard, shadowing their top sales person around for two days to learn the ropes. On my own time, I read different sales books to learn even more. Before long, they let me work on my own and I started having great success.

After three months, they moved me over to the elite team, which was given the biggest prospects. I even got David a job there so we could both cash in. But he wasn't nearly as good at sales as I was and eventually he moved back to what he knew best: pushing boxes in a warehouse. But I was bringing home more money than I'd ever made in my entire life, selling phone line services to major corporations.

David and I were enjoying the increase in our finances and we spent like we were trying to make up for lost time. We bought new clothes, furniture, and took vacations. We even helped out loved ones, gave generously to our church, and put some money away into CDs and retirement plans. We thought the good times would never come to an end.

Baby Blues

During this time, a miracle occurred: I finally got pregnant and didn't have a miscarriage. Because I was considered a high-risk pregnancy, the doctors did extensive blood work on me and the results were not encouraging. I was told my baby would either be stillborn or have Down Syndrome. I knew in my heart I was destined to be a mother and I didn't want to accept what I was being told.

As a step of faith, I went ahead and turned a spare bedroom into a full-blown nursery. I'd take time every day to sit in that room in a rocking chair, praying, singing, speaking over my womb, and calling on the promises of God.

I even refused to get an ultrasound, because I was determined to love my baby regardless. I was so tired of being told my baby wasn't going to be good enough, but eventually the doctor and David got it through my thick head that it would be good to be prepared for whatever problems our child might have. At eight months, not even knowing the gender of the baby, we scheduled the first ultrasound for the following week.

That Sunday we went to church, but we didn't share what was going on with the pregnancy with anyone. The Bishop called me up and gave me a profound word.

"I don't care what the doctors are telling you," he said, "this is a healthy baby and you're going to come back with a good report."

David and I took great comfort in this, but we still had to get through that dreaded ultrasound.

When we showed up for the appointment, the technician first made sure the baby was even alive. I had noticed I wasn't feeling the baby kick like I had before, and I tried not to expect the worse. After trying to get a good reading for a while, the technician left the room and came back with the doctor. That's never a good sign.

Their faces were very calm and professional, but both David and I were about to explode with the stress.

Eventually, the doctor looked at me and asked, "Who told you this baby was stillborn?"

I told him my doctor had run some blood work that came back questionable. He shook his head and pointed my attention to the monitor screen.

"Do you see this baby's hands?"

And I could see that they were moving quickly.

"Stillborn babies have webbed hands. They can't move that way."

And in a very calm voice he said, "Honey, you have a healthy baby boy. Nothing's wrong with him."

As soon as the doctor said those words, David fell on the floor in a heap of tears. We were both so relieved and so emotional because all the tension that had been building up over our complicated pregnancy had been completely undone.

We named our son Valentino, or Tino for short. His name means "valiant one" and the words of promise, hope, and a blessed future I spoke over him while I rocked him in my womb are the same words I speak over him today. I know when he grows up he will make his own choices. But I firmly believe that the words I speak over him will come to pass as he fulfills his own divine destiny.

The Crash X 2

Right about the time Valentino was born, the 2008 recession began. We couldn't see a real difference at first, but over time I noticed that my paychecks, though still large, were beginning to get smaller. Sometimes I was sure I should have been paid more, but it wasn't showing up in my check.

We'd had such a complicated pregnancy with Valentino, we didn't know if we should be daring enough to try to have a baby again. But to our surprise, when Tino was 10 months old, we discovered that a little girl was already baking in my oven. With another pregnancy, I stopped thinking so much about the recession and turned my attention to my growing belly. I didn't have the complications this time, and I enjoyed preparing for our next child.

Little Tino was growing like a weed. One day, during a well visit, the doctor asked how tall Tino's father was. When I told him 6'4", the doctor said that explained Tino's unusual growth chart and that I shouldn't be surprised if it seemed like Tino actually grew overnight. I didn't think much about it at the time. I knew my own belly seemed to be growing overnight, as I was by now over halfway through my pregnancy.

As Tino had gotten older, we'd baby-proofed everything in sight as he began to crawl and then walk. Outlet covers, gates, you name it, we did it. I didn't want him to get exposed to bad germs either, so I always made sure to sanitize his pacifier in boiling water.

The easy way to do it was to heat up a mug of water in the microwave, pop his pacifier in it, and let it sit in the microwave. Later I'd take it out and set it on the counter until it was completely cool. I always made sure to put the mug far back from the edge, so little Tino, who was now 1 ½ years old, couldn't reach it.

It was the day after Tino's latest well visit and David and I were in the kitchen. I had sanitized Tino's pacifier as usual, let it sit in the microwave for a long time before I set it out, like always, on the counter to finish cooling.

David and I were there in the kitchen, not cooking or doing anything in particular, and I was just waiting on Tino's pacifier to finish cooling so I could give it to him. Tino was with us, but I wasn't concerned, because Tino couldn't reach the counter. Or at least he couldn't reach it the day before.

I turned my back to Tino to go to the sink and the next thing I heard was the mug shattering on the tile floor, followed by a thud and the sound of crying. I jerked around to realize that Tino had gotten on his little tippy toes, hooked his pinky finger through the mug handle, and poured the water all over his face and down onto his chest. He'd slipped and fallen in the process, and we thought his screaming was because he'd been hurt in the fall.

My first instinct was to make sure he wasn't cut by the broken mug, but he looked fine. David thought Tino was just startled, but I knew something about his cry wasn't right. Something else was wrong. David was calm at this point, but I was freaking out.

"I think the water was too hot!" I cried.

David said, "It can't be. It's been sitting there forever."

But all I could think was that he had been burned by the water and I needed to pour cold water onto him immediately. The sink in the kitchen was too full to do it there, so I picked him up under his two arms and rushed him upstairs to the bathtub. I poured cold water over him as quickly as I could. In my rush, I took off his little pants but didn't think to take off his t-shirt. His crying got a little better at first, and I hoped we'd seen the worst of this little drama. But it was not to be.

His cry got worse and worse. I knew we had to get him to the hospital and fast. David still wasn't convinced anything major was wrong, but he wasn't going to argue with a very pregnant woman who was freaking out. I didn't want to put Tino in a car seat in his hysterical state, so I literally held him under his arms in front of me as we sped our way to the ER.

Both Tino and I were inconsolable and David was just trying to maintain sanity at this point. And as we were driving, my worst fears came true before my eyes. Water blisters began forming all over little Tino's face and body.

My heart wrenched within me as I thought to myself, "Oh my God! What have I done to my baby?"

My mind instantly filled with "what if's" and indescribable guilt. With all the safety measures we'd put in place, how could a little cup of water cause so much damage? But the worst was yet to come.

When we got to the hospital, the staff could see that we were both in a terrible state. They were concerned that I would go into early labor because I was so emotionally out of control. They quickly took Tino from my arms. But as they took him from me, I noticed that Tino's baby skin had come off onto my hands. I can still remember the smell of his damaged flesh. It was absolutely horrible, and any mother's worst nightmare.

Tino was admitted to the hospital and put into a morphine bath for the pain. He was totally disfigured; all you could see through the dressings on his face was one eye that was so swollen he couldn't see through it. Naturally, I was still very distraught when the doctors came in to talk with us. They said if I hadn't put him under the cold water, his condition would have been so much worse. But my quick actions had turned off the heat.

"You saved his face," one doctor told us.

When I looked at Tino, who was now sedated, all I could see were bandages and his head that was swelling to what looked like twice the normal size. But the doctor was very optimistic and assured me that in three weeks, Tino's skin would be almost back to normal. I thought that the doctor was lying, but I hoped he was right.

He also explained something else. He told me that the water in that mug would not have been hot enough to burn adult skin. Because baby skin was so thin, it was, but there was no way I could have known that. I was thankful for his words, but the guilty feelings remained.

My bosses at the telecom company were very understanding. They told me to take off as much time as I needed so I could care for my son. They even offered to help pay for any bills I couldn't cover. For about a month my full-time job became taking care of Tino. And let me tell you, it wasn't easy for either of us.

The worst part of Tino's treatment was the salt water baths to remove the dead skin. Later, they attached synthetic skin to his wounds and I watched his body heal as the new and the old skin became one.

Even in this difficult time, there were little blessings to see us through. Tino's favorite movie, *The Adventures of Elmo in Grouchland,* just happened to be playing on the TV when the nurses changed his bandages. One of the nurses on the floor was one of our neighbors and although Tino couldn't see her, he recognized her voice. Another sweet friend from church came by to visit and sang Tino lovely lullaby songs and he fell asleep in my arms.

Once we got out of the hospital, we had to keep coming back to get his bandages changed. After two weeks, it still looked to me like my baby would be scarred for life. However, by three weeks, Tino looked amazingly better. You could see the two different skins, and his new skin was red and lighter. But at least he had skin and it was healthy.

In order for his skin to heal properly, the doctors told us to keep him completely out of the sun for a year. Our large downstairs living area was transformed into an indoor playground so Tino wouldn't have to miss out on being a normal kid. While today Tino says he doesn't even remember this painful experience, for me, it remains the most traumatic thing I've ever had to go through. But unfortunately, it wouldn't be the last.

Out of the Frying Pan and into the Fire

With Tino well into recovery, our daughter, Natalia, was born. Our sweet baby girl's name means "born on the Lord's Day." She was such a sweet, happy baby right from the start.

One day after returning to work, I was sitting at my desk and the phone rang. It was David calling from his warehouse job, but something didn't sound right. He said he was having severe chest pain and he thought he was having a heart attack. I said, "If you're having a heart attack, why are you calling me? Call 911! Don't waste your time calling me. Call for an ambulance!"

He said he'd already asked, but his supervisors wouldn't call for one. David just needed my reassurance that he needed to get out of there immediately and seek medical help.

David hung up, decided that he couldn't wait any longer, and drove himself to the hospital instead. He told me later the pain was so bad he heard voices in his head saying, "Just run yourself into a pole and end it quicker!"

Somehow, by the grace of God, he managed to make it to the ER. The staff there confirmed that David was indeed suffering from a heart attack.

I joined David at the hospital where he was diagnosed with Kawasaki Disease, a rare disorder that affects the heart's blood vessels in certain children. Left untreated, it can cause heart attacks in young adults, just like David. Because he was a 70s' baby, this issue wasn't diagnosed when he was younger. He was in his 30s before the problem became apparent.

The doctors told him that he needed complete bed rest to recover. He couldn't even lift more than five pounds at a time. I was so grateful that he was alive, but his heart attack brought a host of new worries. I had two babies in diapers and my best friend could die. Now what? Were my children going to be fatherless? Would I become a statistic?

I was scared about what the future held and uncertain how we'd make it financially. I couldn't quit my job and stay home to take care of my husband, Tino, and Natalia, because I was the only one who could bring home a paycheck.

Thankfully, over time, a combination of traditional and holistic medicine, along with prayer and divine intervention, helped David make a full recovery. But that would take a while. In the short term, David would need to take a leave of absence from his job and stay home to recover.

The Other Shoe Drops and My Cake Journey Begins

Our family was growing, but my paycheck was shrinking. The recession was taking its toll and rumors of trouble in the company got louder and louder. I was still employed for the time being, but I was beginning to realize this job might not last forever. Coworkers were being laid off, but I was a little cocky and thought that because I was one of their best sales people, they wouldn't let go of me. Even though I remained a top performer, my paychecks had dwindled to the point that we already had to dip into savings to make ends meet.

During all this uncertainty, I was sitting with my friend during lunch one day, the one from the nail salon that had introduced me to my current job in the first place. Sitting and talking about our future goals was the norm for us. During lunch breaks, we'd sit down and create business ideas and opportunities that we wanted to venture into and dream of what life could be like in the next five years.

She said, "Hey, I know a gal who makes amazing cakes, and she teaches at the Michael's craft store down the street."

We thought, why not go there after work and take a cake class? We did art design on itty bitty nails. We could do it on a bigger canvas. To be honest, I wasn't too excited about it, but she convinced me to sign up and just do it for fun. We booked the class together for the following week.

But before the week was over, she came up to me and said, "Elaine, I think they're going to fire me. I just hope they let me do unemployment."

She thought they might let her go because she didn't always show up to work after she'd earned big commissions. But the truth was that the company was downsizing and my friend could sense the tension. I reassured her that everything would be OK, but I was really trying to reassure myself. As much money as I made for this company, how could they let me go?

My friend's instincts were correct and she was let go by the end of the week. She was so upset about it, she told me that she didn't want to go to the cake class anymore, so I arranged to bring a niece instead. Just because my friend lost her job didn't mean I couldn't do something for fun.

The next week, the day of the cake class arrived. I brought all the supplies I would need for the class and had arranged for David to be home with the babies. The work day was almost over, but right before it was time to leave, my boss called me into his office. My heart sank. A part of me knew what was coming but a part of me highly doubted they'd let me go.

My boss said, "I'm sorry, but our company is downsizing. Business just isn't what it used to be and we're trying to keep the employees who have been here the longest. So we're going to let you go. We'll give you unemployment, at least, since we know you have children at home to support. You're an amazing sales person, but this is just how it has to be."

All I could say at the time was, "Thank you."

I held my head up high and expressed my appreciation for the opportunity they'd given me and also for the unemployment. But it was all I could do to keep it together as I walked out of the building for the last time.

I got in my car and just cried. At this point, I hit rock bottom. My mind quickly ran the numbers of my mortgage, electric bill and other expenses. My pay was going to drop from a high of $10,000 a month to $250 a week. David was still recovering from his heart attack, and the recession was in full swing. I wouldn't be able to find another job like the one I'd just left. Nobody could. How could we possibly make it? How was I going to tell David what had happened?

I suddenly remembered that before I was going home, I was supposed to attend the cake class. I was very upset, but I decided to go anyway. I really didn't want to go home and share the bad news. I wanted to put that off for a few more hours. I got my niece and we went to the class.

The instructor started the class by having us introduce ourselves. When my turn came, I heard myself saying, "My name is Elaine and I just lost my job. I am here to reinvent myself. This is my new business."

The teacher looked at me like I was crazy and I guess I was. The eternal optimist in me wasn't dead and I was looking for something to hang on to.

That evening, we made a little happy face cake, though I must confess my cake looked like it had the flu instead. When I showed it to David, he wasn't impressed. He told me to stick to my day job. I had to tell him I didn't have a day job anymore. This cake "business" I had decided to start was all we had, plus $250 a week in unemployment. It took a little while for our serious situation to sink in to him.

Hungry Season #2

Financial survival mode kicked in and I knew what to do. I was able to do nails, though it was a drop in the bucket when it came to covering our bills. We hunkered down and cut our expenses as much as we could. Thanks to the crash of the housing bubble, we started the process of modifying our sky-high mortgage and didn't have to make that payment for a while.

Income from a rental property helped out, along with handouts from family. My sister would come by and see our empty fridge, then bring us bags of much needed groceries. Other times diapers would appear on our doorstep. David and I would go to visit our mothers on the weekends, hoping they would cook for us so at least the kids could eat.

Other unexpected blessings helped us keep our heads above water. A mortgage settlement check showed up in the mail. An overpay refund we knew nothing about came in. Our parents helped out as much as they could. We were getting by, but the struggle was real. David decided that even though he was still recovering from his heart attack, he couldn't wait the full year to go back to work. It hurt me to see him return to his warehouse job where he pushed boxes in 100-degree heat, but we had to do what we could to survive.

One priceless benefit of this season was that I got to enjoy my children and spend time with them. I had always had the desire to do so, and now that I didn't have a regular job anymore, I was able to be with them most of the time. I will never regret those precious days spent with them when they were so young.

This season was a very humbling one for me. I had to go and sign up for WIC so the kids could be cared for and there I saw an entirely different society than I was accustomed to. Here I was, with years of excellent credit and a three-year history of making incredible money and now I was filling out forms to apply for public aid. Even though it was painful, the process was the best thing that could have happened to me. My pride was jacked up, but I needed that humbling. I needed to be broken so I could be molded into a better person.

An Enticing Reinvention

I continued my little cake class, but this time with great focus and intent. David thought I was crazy and I can't blame him based on the quality of what I was bringing home. I got so mad at him for being critical and not being more supportive, when all I was doing was trying to learn a new trade so I could put food on the table.

But the anger wasn't really about him. I had to prove to myself, again, that I wasn't going to starve, that I was going to make it, and that I was going to turn this around. I'd made it through setbacks before and I would make it through this one, too.

Cake decorating became an obsession with me. As I had in past seasons when starting a new chapter, I consumed everything I could find on the subject: magazines, blogs, tutorials, cookbooks, videos, and television shows. I clipped my 50% off coupons like clockwork and marched down to the local Michael's craft store on a regular basis to buy more decorating tools and supplies. I figured those cashiers knew me by name because I was in there so often.

I wanted to get good enough to sell at least one cake, so I would pick one technique and master it. Then I would move on to another technique and master that one. I knew I didn't have to learn it all at once. I just knew I had to get better. And I gave myself three months to learn and start selling cakes.

I took that very first cake class in July, 2010, and by October I made my first birthday cake for my godson's party. In November 2010, I made a Hello Kitty cake for our daughter Nati's first birthday. I really worked hard to impress and to this day, I can't find one flaw on that cake. From that point on, I was officially on my way in my new cake business, which I named Enticing Cake Boutique. I gradually began making cakes for hire and my skills continued to improve.

One of the cake shows I watched was a new baking and cake competition show by TLC called *Next Great Baker*, a spin-off of the popular *Cake Boss* show featuring Carlos Bakery and Buddy Valastro. I watched Dana Herbert win Season 1.

My sister knew I was on a cake adventure and she told me, "You know, you're good enough to be on that show."

I said, "You're crazy. I'm not that good yet. But one day, if I can get on that show, I'll know I have arrived."

My sister believed in me more than I believed in myself at that point and she brought me the application to apply for Season 2. She told me, "You're going to get on that show."

I still thought she was crazy, and so did David, and I knew I was still wet behind the ears. But I was a risk taker and I'd try anything once. I submitted the application.

One day the phone rang and the voice on the other end said, "Hello, this is High Noon Entertainment."

I thought I was getting punked so I hung up on them. Then I looked at the caller ID. Oops. It really WAS them.

I sheepishly called them back and the lady said, "It's OK. That's not the first time that's happened."

She let me know that I was still in the running and how they wanted me to continue the audition process. Weeks went by, but as the cast was chosen for Season 2, my name was not on the list. I was disappointed, but just the fact that they had actually considered me lit me up to push into my cake journey even harder.

Taking It to the Next Level

Over the next year, my cake business grew as my skills improved and I tapped into the cake industry. I developed a social media presence and a basic website. I sold cakes to people I knew and offered cake tastings to my neighbors. Though I wasn't able to charge as much as I wanted for my cakes, at least I was making money and was feeling accomplished. I met a photographer who started taking pictures of my creations and submitting them to local magazines. This led to my cake pictures showing up in blogs, other magazines, and places I couldn't have imagined.

Season 3 of the *Next Great Baker* came up and, once again, I was considered for the show. And once again, the answer was no. I was disappointed, of course, but by now I had connected to the wedding industry and I was getting real orders for my cakes. I'd learned how to stack cakes so they wouldn't fall over, more advanced decorating skills, and the business side of the catering world from a friend who showed me the ropes. I went to the local wedding shows and turned to the local Chamber of Commerce to educate myself even more.

Through referrals, I saw a slow but steady increase in my cake business. All my cake money went to pay bills and David continued his warehouse job. Our mortgage was still being modified, so not having a house payment for a time was a huge help. Our grocery bills were down to $50 a week. We were getting by, but it was still a struggle.

Even though *Next Great Baker* didn't want me, I still pursued the cake industry recognition I was hungry for. *Cake Central Magazine* had a special collector's book coming out called *Cake Adore 2013* that featured some of the best cake artists in the world and only 500 copies were to be sold worldwide.

As I saw the announcement for the issue to come, I thought to myself, "I'd love to be in that issue. What an honor that would be."

I had posted many of my cakes on their website and I would have given anything to be included in that issue. As time went by, I actually got a little disappointed that this was one dream that wasn't going to come true. I had poured so much energy into reinventing myself as a cake decorator and I wanted the affirmation to confirm I had made it.

I was looking through my email one day and noticed one I had looked over before. I just assumed it was another Cake Central daily email featuring different design ideas, as usual. But when I clicked on it, it said something far different. It was a notice to let me know I had been chosen for their first collector's book ever published: *Cake Adore 2013*. I couldn't believe it. Yet another little dream had come true. I was so proud when my harvest cake appeared in the limited hard cover addition, alongside amazing cakes from all over the world.

But one big dream remained: getting on *Next Great Baker.* *Season 4* rolled around and I wasn't sure I wanted to apply again. I'd already been rejected two times before. At first, in my own mind, I had tied my cake success to getting on this show and using that exposure to get me to the next level. But I'd realized my cake business could still be successful; it would just take a longer path to get there. Nevertheless, I decided to give it one more go.

I got a call from the show saying that I was being considered, but Season 4 would feature teams instead of individual bakers. David agreed to be my sidekick and we continued through the audition process.

As we anxiously awaited their decision, I thought back over all the years of struggle that had led me to this point. Less than five years before, I had started my cake journey. I'd grown so much over such a short period of time. Was this finally going to be the big break we were waiting for?

Elaine, You're "Next!"

Finally, the phone call came. Yes, we had made it - we, not just me. David, my best friend and the man who had looked at my first sad "happy face" cake and told me to stick with my day job, was now going to be my cake partner on national television. We would be the only husband and wife team on the show.

David made sure he was going to support me no matter what. He was floored that I had set out on an ambitious journey that was now unfolding before our very eyes.

He apologized to me, saying, "If I ever seemed like I doubted you, honey, I am sorry. I will never do that again."

He always says he's my biggest fan. And he is.

We were so excited, but we had some hard choices to make as well. Our finances were still very tight. How were we going to make ends meet while we were away for filming? And we'd never left our babies before. Especially after what had happened to Tino when he was little, we liked to keep our children close. We were able to make arrangements with our family to care for them in our absence. Saying goodbye to them was one of the hardest things we had ever had to do.

Our time in Buddy's Lackawanna Bakery was one of the highlights of our lives. We made lots of great friends as we competed our way through each episode. We didn't get started well out of the gate, serving raw cake batter to the judges in the very first challenge because we weren't quite sure how to work their super high-tech ovens. When we put our cake into that fancy oven, we were confident it was already on, but we were wrong. That was so embarrassing.

But before our time was over, we were able to show the judges and America not just our cake skills, but also the genuine love David and I had for each other. Our best moment from the show was when we won the Carrabba's

Dessert Challenge and had our Duran's Divine Pineapple Pound Cake named after us and served in Carrabba's restaurants around the country.

Being on the show was incredibly rewarding, but also incredibly stressful. We were surrounded by amazing cake artists and bakers, and competing alongside them was an honor for which I am so thankful. And I'm thankful to the Cake Boss himself for giving all of us a chance to show our skills on an international stage. But all good things must come to an end, and after five episodes we were eliminated as competitors, though we did get return for the final reunion episode.

After the show aired, we received lots of attention locally and even around the world, as people sent us messages of how much they'd enjoyed watching us on the show. I can honestly say that the love people witnessed between David and I wasn't just for the camera. It was real. It still is. David and I are one. After all the struggles we've been through together, nothing can tear us apart. David and I can sit and talk for hours about our sweet moments, heart-breaking seasons, and our comeback victories.

Not A Magic Wand

Just because we made it on the show, our financial troubles were not over. Not by any means. People would see us and think we were super successful, but they didn't know that our mortgage was still being modified and we had to dip into our retirement to meet our expenses. And while my cake business got a boost, being on television was by no means a magic wand that made all my cake dreams come true. I would still need to work it hard and keep my nose to the grindstone.

Open Doors, Opened Hearts

Several doors opened for us after being on the show. One was to be guest celebrity chefs at home shows. The organizers had seen us on TV and they wanted us travel to the different shows, do live cake demonstrations, and share a little about what it was like to be on *Next Great Baker*. David and I weren't sure exactly what to say in our presentation, but we knew that we'd always wanted to have an inspirational platform. How could we use this opportunity to inspire people to follow their dreams?

We arrived at our first home show and we had to do three presentations that day. The first one was a hot mess. Our nerves got the best of us. We felt like we were rambling, and ended up just mainly talking about our experience on TV and expressing thanks for being at the home show. Before the second show, we knew we had to change it up. We wanted to hold the audience's attention and not have them get up and leave in the middle like they did in our first presentation. We decided to tell our own story, not just the TV story.

"It doesn't matter if you're a mechanic or a teacher or a janitor, but it's about how great a mechanic or teacher or janitor you can be," I told them.

David and I went on to encourage them to be the best at whatever they were doing and to follow their dreams. The crowd stayed glued to their seats and carefully listened to every word we said.

Another Stage

A line formed after our talk so that people could shake our hands and thank us for the encouraging message we'd shared. Two of them were Chefs Collen Engle and Jesse Vazquez, from the Miami Culinary Institute. Our message had resonated deeply with them and Jesse was deeply moved.

"Our students need to hear this message," he said.

He explained that many of their students had come from either third world countries or urban environments and had studied at the school so they could have a better life.

"Would you be willing to be the keynote speaker to our graduates at our next Chef Coat Ceremony?" he asked.

David and I were quite surprised. Who would want to hear our story? Why did people think it was so phenomenal? I guess when it happens to you and it's your story, it doesn't seem as special. Then we realized it wasn't about us. It was about the divine purpose in our lives.

David and I weren't anyone famous. We didn't even win the title of Next Great Baker. But the message of hope, perseverance, and going for your dreams was a message that everyone not just wanted to hear, but needed to hear. And David and I were so blessed to share it. We decided since I was the loud-mouth in the family, I'd be the one to do the talking.

When we went to Miami for the Chef Coat Ceremony, we felt like winners in the eyes of the faculty, staff, and students there. The speaker before me was a multi-millionaire and the owner of a very successful brewery. After he spoke, I wasn't sure how my humble story would stack up to his. But I gained confidence as Chef Collen Engle began his introduction.

"In the beginning, David was a warehouse worker and he lost his job after suffering a heart attack in 2010. Elaine switched into what she calls 'survival mode' at that time, which included a lot of baking. A cake decorating class led to a call from TLC and an offer to appear in *Next Great Baker's* fourth season.

"They competed against nine other teams and David and Elaine made over-the-top desserts, like a Paris themed wedding cake and a 600 pound 6 ft. high candy tower, which I can't even imagine. But they were eliminated in the fifth episode during a scary ingredient challenge where they had to add bleu cheese to a red velvet cake." Chef Engle laughed at the thought of it before he went on. "The Duran's had won the Carrabba's Dessert Challenge the week before, though, and that placed their Duran's Divine Pineapple Pound Cake in 240 of the chain's restaurants for a limited time.

"The flamboyant Kissimmee couple run an online cake business called Enticing Cake Boutique and have been known to sport leopard cuff tunics and create cakes with purple rhinestones and gold leaf. 'Never a boring cake' is their motto. Elaine says the next dream is to open their own shop. 'Our high,' Elaine says, 'was being on the show and winning that challenge.' Their low was 'going home before the finale. But hard always pays off.'"

As Chef Engle wrapped up his introduction, I glanced over to David and whispered, "Is he talking about us?"

At that moment the weight of our journey fell on my soul. Did we really do all those things, in less than five years? Yes, we had. Our seasons of deep disappointment had turned into the life we had been destined to live. Chef Engle's final words broke into my thoughts.

"So here to tell you more about their journey are Elaine and David. Please welcome them to the stage."

As I took a deep breath and made my way to the podium, I knew I wasn't just stepping onto the stage at the Miami Culinary Institute. I was stepping out onto the stage of my destiny. While this was not the highest point of my life, it was a very important milestone on my journey.

The same courage, perseverance, and faith that had brought me this far would also see me through to the next level and the ones beyond. And I knew I had a life-changing message to share, not only to those new graduates, but to the world: our struggles, failures, and losses can be turned into lives filled with hope, joy, and purpose. And if it happened to me, it can happen to you. Your stage is waiting. It's your turn now. *You're Next!*

PART TWO

Introduction

Well, that's my life story — but not really. My journey, like yours, is ongoing. Who knows what the future will hold, what joys and what struggles lie ahead? One of the unique things about this book is that it's written by someone who is in the trenches with you. I hope my story can inspire you in your journey, but I hope by now you see that I'm far from perfect and nothing has ever been given to me on a silver platter.

I'm even more excited about the second part of the book you're about to read. Anyone can turn their disappointment into destiny, but there are some basic principles you need to follow. I will give you the keys that have helped me — and keep helping me — through my many struggles. And believe me, I still have struggles. In fact, I'm keeping a copy of this book around so I can remind myself of how to stay on track when I'm tempted to get discouraged or distracted. Destiny-making is hard work but it IS possible. And the payoff is priceless. Remember, if I can do it, anyone can.

I want to say right now that I do not consider myself an expert in these areas, though just like I have in other areas of my life, I have consumed a lot of books and teachings on how to get and stay motivated. Many of these truths are so ingrained in me they are second nature by now and I honestly couldn't give you the source of each one. In the back of the book I've put a list together of helpful resources if you want to go deeper than I have in these pages. So, are you ready to start turning your disappointment into the destiny you've always wanted? Then turn the page, because You're Next!

6

EVERYONE HAS A
PURPOSE AND DESTINY

Over the next few chapters, we are going to get into the specifics of how you can turn your disappointment into destiny. We'll discuss what a destiny is and some basic principles that are true for all of us. I'll show you the greatest barrier to your destiny and how you can overcome it. Together we'll unlock the secret to moving forward, learn how to keep the momentum going, and help you create a new and achievable definition of success. That's a lot of ground to cover, so let's get started.

Defining Terms

Before we go any further, let's define a few specific terms: destiny, purpose, dreams, and calling. These words relate to each other, though they are slightly different in meaning. In simplest terms, destiny is the unique journey or path of your life. Purpose is the reason you're on the path in the first place. Dreams are the goals you have along this path. And calling is the role or roles you play along the way.

Destiny is the place where your purpose, dreams, and calling connect and come into motion. When I say the word "destiny," I mean the fulfilled life you were born to live, which is a result of the combination of your purpose, calling, and dreams. If your destiny seems to be in a "stuck" mode, most likely there's a disconnect somewhere between your purpose, dreams, and/or calling.

Your purpose is your motivation. It's what empowers and gives you direction in your life. It's the "why" you do what you do. Your calling is a mixture of your natural bents, the talents and gifts you were born with, and the skills you develop. Your dreams are the desires and goals you have because of the purpose that motivates you and the calling you want to fulfill. True dreams are the natural fruit of your purpose and your calling.

Let me use my own life as an example. My life purpose is to be the best that I can be in every area of my life by using the God-given gifts and talents I have, so that I can bless others along the way. My calling is that of a mother and a wife, and also a creative artist, encourager, and communicator. My natural bent is that of an optimist, exhorter and entrepreneur. I have gifts in art and I've developed skills in design and cake decorating.

My dreams are many, but here a few: I want to speak to others on an inspirational platform and inspire them to fulfill their own unique destiny. I want to have my own brick and mortar shop where I can help create memories and sell our great cakes. I want to create a legacy for my children and teach them to be intentional about following their own dreams.

My destiny is where my combined purpose, calling, and dreams all come into alinement and bring about the fulfilled life I've always wanted. Destiny is not a destination; it is a journey. Destiny is not a finish line, because destiny is almost an ongoing feeling of arrival at the perfect time in the perfect place in the perfect season. However, it moves with you because as your dreams expand, so does your destiny.

Walking in your destiny isn't like being a piece of driftwood on the cosmic ocean, getting pushed into the next season of your life against your will. It's actually quite the opposite. Destiny demands your activity. It demands your focused participation. A destiny doesn't come to pass without your involvement. And sadly, very few people fulfill their destiny. But that doesn't have to be your story. And if you put the principles I'm sharing into action, it won't.

We'll talk more about all these terms as we go. But now that you know what I mean by destiny, let's take a look at the title of my book. *You're Next: Turn Your Disappointment into Destiny* assumes a few things. First, it assumes you'd like to be "next," that you'd like to have your turn at success. I doubt too many people would say no to that. It also assumes that you've had some disappointments along the way. Is there anybody reading this who hasn't had a least of few of those? I've yet to meet anyone who's had a problem-free life. My title also assumes that you have a destiny you'd like to fulfill.

A $20 Bill

But there's no need for me to talk more about destiny unless you think you are valuable enough to have one. Some people have so little self-worth they don't think they should have anything. But I am firmly convinced that every living person has value. You are valuable. You are precious. You have priceless worth. It doesn't matter how much money you have, the level of your education, or the color of your skin. You are a person of worth.

Maybe you've heard the story about a teacher who wanted to teach his students a lesson about the value of money. He held up a brand new $20 bill in his hand and asked if anyone wanted it. Of course, every hand shot up. He wrinkled the money into a wad and asked if anyone wanted it. Again, every hand was raised. He went on to step on the $20 bill, to draw on it, and finally, grind it into the ground. But every time, every hand went up, wanting that $20 bill.

Why did they still want it? Because the worth of the bill never changed. It kept its value, regardless of its condition. The same is true of you. It doesn't matter if you're wrinkled, dirty, or ripped right down the middle. It doesn't matter what's in your past or what skeletons are hiding in your closet. It doesn't matter if someone told you that you wouldn't amount to anything. It doesn't matter how many times you've failed or how many mistakes you've made. Just like that $20 bill, your value hasn't changed. Sure, other people may not value you, but that does NOT make you worthless. It just shows their ignorance.

Created for Greatness

You were created with value and you were created with a destiny. Even if you doubt that, you can't deny that there are dreams you've always had that you wish would come true. Even as a child, you saw your future and dreamed of great things to come. You were created for greatness. You were born to dream. That's why that desire is in you. You didn't make it up. Your life has a purpose. And it's not too late to find it.

From birth, you've been hard-wired a certain way. Maybe your gifts are hard for other people to understand, but there is a reason you are put together the way you are. You were born with these things; you didn't just develop them later. Every parent knows that even in the womb each of their children are unique. And boy, once they come out, you know it for sure! Kids are not these little blank slates just waiting for us to tell them who to be.

Some aspects of your destiny may not become obvious until years down the road. I never thought I'd be on national television doing cake competitions. But the seeds of that experience were in me at birth: my creativeness, my love for art, my confident and competitive personality. Even if you aren't sure what your life purpose is, don't worry. Most of us need try more than a few doors before we find the one that's just right for us. The important thing is keep knocking.

It's Not Just About You

Another important fact about destiny is that it's not just about you. When you feel as though you are on the right path to fulfilling your destiny, you want to bring everybody along with you on the journey. You want to bless along the way, because you've found an avenue of inner success that you can't contain all by yourself. As you walk down the path of your destiny, you will help others reach theirs.

Do you remember when I took my very first cake class the day I lost my job, where I boldly said I was reinventing myself and this was my new business? The teacher of the class contacted me years later, after she'd seen my appearance on *Next Great Baker*. She told me she was so inspired by my journey that she had found the courage to step out into her own dreams, and eventually opened her own high-end furniture store. Sure, someone or something else might have inspired her, but it was my journey that provided the spark that set her unfulfilled dreams aflame.

We hear all the time about looking out for #1, making sure you get yours, forcing our way to the top and the take-no-prisoners approach to business. But a true destiny doesn't work that way. It's about being generous — not just with your money, but with your advice and encouragement. I'm so thankful for the people who encouraged me along my path or gave me an opportunity, like my Grandpa Oscar, or I wouldn't be where I am today.

What is Your Destiny?

Do you know what your destiny is? Some people can answer that question without any hesitation. But many people are still unsure. They're still searching for clarity and definition to that inner longing that leaves them hoping for more. For those who need help in uncovering their unique destiny, here are a few questions to consider:

What are you passionate about?
What makes you come alive inside?
What are your natural talents and abilities?
What skills have you developed?
What makes you tick?
What are your greatest strengths?
What would you do if money was not an issue?
What were your childhood dreams?
Did someone along the way discourage you from following a dream, and yet that desire still burns inside you?

If any of these questions resonated with you, take a few minutes and jot down your answers. You might find a pattern beginning to take shape that will help you define your destiny.

You might even want to ask those closest to you how they would answer those questions about you. Sometimes others can see our qualities better than we can.

Don't Take Your Destiny with You!

There's an old phrase that says, "You can't take it with you." And one thing you don't want to take with you to the grave is your destiny. The sad fact is that most people die with their dreams still inside them. Graveyards are filled with unmet desires, delayed dreams, and unrealized potential. It shouldn't be that way. Why should we expire before we can inspire? We must not lose our desire and our hunger for abundant life.

Why is it so rare that people fulfill their destiny? You don't have to encourage a child to dream, do you? They're just filled with hope for their future. But along the way, something happens to our dreams. Over time, they are slowly stolen, killed, or destroyed. We suffer wounds from loss or trauma. Those around us shoot down our dreams, or a bad environment makes dreaming seem pointless.

I have made it a point over the years to encourage my own kids to keep dreaming. Every morning on the way to school, I ask Valentino and Natalia, "Why are you here?"

And they say, "To learn and make a difference."

This has been our habit since the first day they started school, because I wanted to inspire them to embrace their education, to increase their knowledge, and grow in their expectation of a purposeful future.

Sometimes our own bad choices put what seem like dream-ending limits on our destiny. Harsh consequences and the resulting guilt and shame cause us to lose hope as we wallow in unworthiness. That's where I found David when we first met. His dreams were so repressed by his past, the only goal he had was to have a working car and rent his own apartment. That was a start, but I knew he was destined for so much more. And so are you. This world isn't known for giving out second chances. But while your actions might not be excusable, they are forgivable. Sometimes the hardest person to give a second chance to is ourselves.

Some dreams just die from neglect, like a house plant you forgot to water or set in a darkened corner. Over time, our dreams wilt and shrivel up until they look like they should be tossed in the garbage can. Dreams must be nurtured. They must be fertilized. Sometimes they need to be pruned, but that's just so the best parts can keep growing. We must protect our dreams from harsh environments and destructive forces. Dreams and destinies must be cared for to blossom and grow.

Why Is Your Destiny on Hold?

Are you living out your destiny? If not, why? What do you think are the reasons your dreams are still waiting to come true? What do you think is the biggest barrier to your destiny?

Before I share with you what that barrier is, I'm going to tell you what it is not. The barrier to your destiny is not your past. I'm so glad our past does not negate our future.

Neither do your mistakes derail your destiny. It's like what happens when you make a wrong turn while using your GPS: a voice says, "Recalculating," or "Re-center; redirecting." Just because you get off track doesn't mean you can't get back on track and still reach your original goal.

You might think that a lack of resources is the main reason your destiny has been delayed. I hope you saw in my life story that a lack of money, education, or time doesn't have to hold you back. You just have to find a way around the roadblocks.

Maybe you think it's just too late for your destiny to come about and old age is the barrier you can't get over. Once again, that's just not true. It's never too late to take back your destiny. There are plenty of people in history who never realized their full potential until the latter years of their lives.

So if your past, your mistakes, your lack of resources, or your age aren't the biggest barriers to your destiny, then what is?

7

THE GREATEST BARRIER TO YOUR DESTINY

Are you ready to discover the greatest barrier to your destiny? Take a look in the mirror, because the biggest barrier to your destiny is *you*. Sorry to tell you that, but it's the truth. For your destiny to be fulfilled, a shift in mindset is required. And that happens right between your two ears. That's where the battleground lies, where the fight for your destiny must occur. And there's not a one of us who doesn't have to break some bad cycles of "stinkin' thinkin'" so we can get out of our rut and onto the road toward the life we want.

Playing the "Blame Game"

The first bad cycle we have to break is what I call the Blame Game. We all play it. Some of us are lifelong experts. By pointing the finger away from ourselves, we shift the responsibility from ourselves and onto other people or things that we can't control. We are no longer accountable for our destiny, because it is no longer our fault that it's not coming to pass. While the Blame Game is a convenient way to excuse us from our stuck state, we've got to stop playing it if we want to move on.

The most common card to play in the Blame Game is the "others" card. We blame our spouse, our significant other, our parents, our brothers and sisters. When those aren't enough, we add in our bosses, teachers, and exes. And these don't have to be people from your present. The Blame Game includes all the people from your past, too. Those are the best, because there's no statute of limitations. You can basically blame them forever, and they can't even talk back.

Another tactic is to blame our past. This huge category includes any difficult events from our childhood, any trauma we've ever endured, as well as our own back luck and bad choices. While I would never belittle the pain or wounds someone carries, the simple fact is that if you stay a victim and use that pain as an excuse to not move forward into your destiny, then you only have yourself to blame. Which by the way, is another card you can play. The "it's-all-my-fault" card has kept multiples of people stuck in their rut of self-pity and shame.

If we don't want to blame our past, we can always blame our present. We can be stuck in all sorts of situations that can appear to keep us from our destiny. Health and weight issues, relationships, living conditions, legal proceedings — the list of possibilities is endless. And new problems will keep arising all the time, so our Blame Game deck always stays fully stacked.

Blaming our lack is another favorite. We lack a proper education and say that's because we lack the brains, the money, or the time to gain one. We lack money to put our dreams into motion. There's just not enough hours in the day to do what it would take to move ahead, because we don't have enough time. We don't have the space and we don't have the tools. We don't have the "right" personality or the "right" opportunity. It's a lot easier to focus on the problem than to keep looking for solutions.

Some blame culture, race, and the prejudice of others. They say, "The deck is just stacked against me, so I can't move forward into my destiny," or "If only 'those' people would stop treating me 'that' way, I could get my piece of the pie." There are true injustices in this world, no doubt. But blaming the ignorance of others won't bring your dreams any closer to reality.

No matter what blame card(s) you've been playing, you must take ownership over your future if you want to live the life you desire. You cannot control other people. You cannot travel back in time and redo the past. You cannot control market cycles, recessions, the weather, or tragic events. You cannot control the time or culture or family into which you were born. The only things you can control are your own choices. You have a free will and you have to be purposeful in how you use it. You are the only one who can choose to be an overcomer.

If a part of your struggle has to do with blaming others, then you've got to let it go. Unforgiveness that isn't dealt with turns into bitterness. And bitterness is like a poison that eats away at your soul, creating all sorts of painful consequences. It's been said that bitterness is like you eating rat poison and then waiting for the rat to die. You aren't harming the other person by not forgiving them; you're only hurting yourself.

Forgiving doesn't mean agreeing that what the other person did to you was fine. It simply means that you aren't going to let the actions of others keep you from having peace of mind and living a life that is whole and free. While you can't control what the other person did, you do get to choose your response. Unfortunately, some choose to hold onto hurts for decades, cheating themselves out of years of peace.

It's easier to forgive others when we realize our need to have others forgive us. No one is perfect and, like me, I'm sure you've made your share of mistakes. Isn't it freeing when others show us mercy when we fall short? Perhaps what was done to you was truly awful. But you don't have to let a painful past steal from your bright future. The great reward when you choose to forgive is mental sanity and mental peace. You owe it to yourself and to the ones you love to walk in forgiveness.

Breaking the Fear Cycle

Another bad cycle of thinking we need to conquer is the matter of fear. When our worries and doubts look larger than our dreams, we won't have the courage to move forward. Fear thrives in the dark. It hides in the corners of our mind, creating all sorts of horrible scenarios that keep our dreams shackled and our destiny trapped. Fear whispers to us in the night, stealing our rest and causing us to dread the day.

Fear tricks us into keeping our worries a secret, because fear knows when it is exposed to the light, its power is greatly diminished. Fear is a thief. It steals your joy, your peace, and your destiny. Fear comes in many faces, but each one is specifically designed to keep you from living the life you were designed to live.

The most common fear is the fear of the unknown. Wouldn't it be nice if we only knew for sure what would happen when we made a certain decision? If we could only predict, with absolute certainty, how much money we'll earn, how well our product will sell, or whether or not we'll get that job we want to apply for? But there's no way to know. And for some of us, it's safer just to sit still and worry than to step forward and take a chance.

I remember stalling in getting my two-year degree because I was afraid the math requirements would be too hard. It was intimidating and I didn't want to face the stress. I wasted almost two years for no other reason than avoiding those classes. When I finally realized I had to finish what I had started and I actually took those dreaded classes, I was mad at myself because they weren't as terrifying as I had thought they would be.

Are there areas in your life you're avoiding because of the fear of the unknown? Is there anything you think might be terrifying, but you don't really know for sure? Are you putting off important decisions because uncertainty is scarier than remaining stuck?

The fear of change is closely related to the fear of the unknown. Sometimes even when you know what will happen, the idea of the change itself is enough to stop you in your tracks. We're comfortable where we're at. Will it be hard to adapt to that new job? What will it look like when I lose the weight and I'm not fat anymore? Will I lose my fat friends and will people expect more of me? To start my new business, am I willing to give up some of my free time to make it successful? We are creatures of habit, but not being willing to change is a habit we must break.

I experienced the fear of change when my ex-husband left me and I was suddenly a young divorcee. I felt abandoned and embarrassed and I didn't want to go out in public. I didn't want people to see me at functions alone. Would they start asking questions I didn't want to answer? Would I feel like a statistic? Would they try to tell me how they thought I should solve my problems? Would they judge me based on what they saw without knowing how hard my marriage was behind closed doors? Such fears would have kept me isolated had I not faced them.

The fear of loss can keep us bound as well. The loss of relationships, of our lifestyle, and the loss of a reliable income are very real concerns. Pursuing our dream may require us delaying our current needs so we can have a bigger reward down the road. But we hesitate to pay the price. The fear of doing without ties into our need for security. And what if we take a risk, come up short, and even end up going backwards? No one wants that.

Another fear that holds us back is the fear of being misunderstood. Will I face ridicule if I pursue my dreams? Will my loved ones understand my choices? What if they don't support me in my decision? What if I'm made fun of because of the path I've chosen?

This was one of my biggest fears while I was teaching myself the art of cake design. My children were still in diapers, so I would put them to bed at night, then sneak off to practice. I was so desperate to learn this new skill that I'd often work until the wee hours of the morning.

Sometimes my daughter would start crying at 3 A.M. while I was covered in buttercream, and it would take a few long minutes for me to clean up so I could console Nati without getting the frosting on her. Sometimes I would rock her back to sleep in one arm while I kept decorating with the other. Tears of frustration would roll down my cheeks because I felt like I was neglecting my children to pursue my dream. But I was in the middle of a project, and if I didn't finish soon, the whole thing would be ruined and I'd have to start over.

I didn't want my children to think I was choosing cake over them, but I knew I had to learn and learn quickly. The feelings from that hard season are still very real to me. I cried a lot in those days because I wanted my dream so badly, but I had to balance my life as a wife and mother, too. Would my family misunderstand my pursuit? Clawing your way up is so difficult.

I would tell myself, "Suck it up Elaine; you've got this!"

But in the midst of the struggle, I certainly had my fears and doubts. Maybe you do, too.

One unique fear that holds some people back is the fear of success. This seems silly at first, because success is the one thing we all want. But once you're successful, you have more demands and expectations to meet. Success requires more of you as a person — more of your time, your maturity, your growth, and relationship skills. Achieving success creates its own set of new stresses and the fear of that keeps some stuck in mediocrity.

What are your fears? What are your greatest worries? What keeps you awake at night and your stomach in a knot during the day? Have you experienced health issues because of your elevated stress level? Are there opportunities you've missed because your fear held you back? What has fear stolen from you in the past and what is it stealing from you today? Here's the most important question of all: are you ready to be free from fear? Are you willing to take steps to stop fear from stealing from you?

Fear can be overcome. And it must be overcome if you want to live a fulfilled life. Overcoming fear is a lot like weeding a flower bed. At the beginning of each spring, you pull up all the weeds. But if you don't mulch well, spray weed killer and pull up weeds as they regrow, your flower bed will look like a jungle before summer is over. Overcoming fear is not a one-time act. It is a continual process we must actively choose if we want to stay free from it.

Weed, Seed, and Feed

To stick with our flower bed illustration, the process to overcome fear can be called the "weed, seed, and feed" method. The first step is to pull up the weeds. This part takes courage, because you actually have to face your fears. You must bring them out of the dark and into the light. Remember when I was pregnant with Valentino and we were told our baby might be either stillborn or have Down Syndrome? Until I brought those fears into the light and had the ultrasound, I wasn't able to be free from my fear. In my case, my fears were unfounded.

Sometimes our secret worries turn out to be true. But isn't it better to find out the truth and deal with the consequences? Many times, when the thing we worried about the most comes to pass, we find out that walking through it wasn't as bad as we expected. We even uncover surprising blessings along the way.

Fear hates being exposed. Fear hates the light. Sometimes just saying our fears out loud helps us realize how silly they are. If you are serious about weeding fear out of your life, I challenge you to write each one down by name. Do it, for real. Naming and exposing our fears begins to break the grip they have on our lives. Trust me; it works.

Once you've clearly defined your fears, the next step is to share them with someone else you trust. If our fears are illogical, our loved one will help us see that. They can help us discover a healthy perspective and a path forward if our fears our founded. They can encourage us on our journey. They might even find the courage to share their fears with you, and you can help each other. Remember, you are wired for connection. Fear wants to keep you isolated because it knows it grows best when you are cut off from others.

The next step in our fear-killer process is to "seed" our mind with the truth. You must make the choice to uncover the actual truth about your specific fears. As you consider each one, are there practical steps you can take to deal with them? You might need to do some research to see if your fear is founded or not. Perhaps you need to make a doctor's appointment. There could be a relationship where you need to discuss your concerns openly. Maybe you need to dig into your bank statements and bills to see the true state of your financial situation. Whatever the fear, there's a strategy to beat it. This reality check displaces your fear and replaces it with facts.

The final step is to "feed" your mind with encouraging truth about yourself and your journey. This is fertilizing the good plants, so the bad plants don't have so much space into which to grow. I'll share more about affirmations later, but for now I'll say that keeping yourself built up on the inside helps limit the number of fears in your life.

Have you read the instructions on a shampoo bottle before? "Lather well, rinse, repeat." It's the same when dealing with fear. Once we weed out our fears by exposing and sharing them, replacing those fears with the seeds of truth, and feeding our souls with encouragement, we find ourselves needing to repeat the process again. Over time you'll find that dealing with weeds when they're just seedlings is much easier than waiting until their roots go down deep and the weeds tower over your head. The good news is that once you get into the "weed, seed, and feed" habit, you'll find that the process is easy to maintain. The fruits of peace, rest, and hope will motivate you to keep at it.

Who are You?

The final bad cycle we'll talk about that needs breaking is the cycle of a false identity. Few people know who they really are. They've been duped into thinking they are worthless, weak, and without purpose. But nothing could be further from the truth. As I explained with the illustration of the $20 bill, your worth doesn't change just because your circumstances do. Your true value isn't based on your accomplishments and it's not diminished by your mistakes. But if you have a negative self-image, then you won't and can't go for your destiny. Destiny-making takes confidence.

Guilt and shame weigh many people down. Guilt says, "I did something wrong." Shame says, "Something is wrong with me." Both are destiny killers. Facing our past mistakes and making restitution where we can are never easy, but once we have done what we can, we need do one more thing: forgive ourselves. We need to love ourselves, just as we are. Living under a cloak of shame sucks all the energy out of our destiny.

Some people have the false identity of not being capable. "I could never do that," they say when viewing someone else's success. But you are capable. You are enough. You have enough to start and your capacity can be increased to attain and sustain your dream. That's certainly been true for me. When I started my cake journey, all I could do was turn out a sad lookin' "happy face" that nobody wanted. But I had enough capability to start, and over time, I became capable of so much more.

Defining ourselves by our experiences and lack is another trap to avoid. When I met David, he saw himself through the lens of a young man who had lived a hard life filled with poverty. But I could see that he had greatness in him. It took time before he saw that greatness in himself. But once he did, he came alive and his life radically changed.

Another powerful aspect about identity is the idea that you are a part of something bigger than yourself. It's not all about you. You are a part of a community. You are wired for connection. You have a family, friends, neighbors, and coworkers. You may associate with a certain faith-based group, social cause, or movement. Even hobbies and athletic pursuits can create a sense of community for us. The important thing to remember is that you are not an island. Your dream and destiny ties into that of others, helping them create and attain theirs.

One of a Kind

So far, what I've talked about with identity is true for all us. We each have value. We are capable and we are enough. Our past doesn't have to define us. We are a part of community that is bigger than ourselves. While there are many similar traits that unite us, we also have an amazing set of gifts, talents, bents, etc. that are unique to us. You are truly one of a kind.

We all have a deep desire to be known and understood. But the first step to meeting that need is for you to truly know and understand yourself. We touched on this briefly in the first chapter when I asked you about your own destiny. So let's go a little bit deeper into the story of *you*. Here's a simple list of areas for you to explore so you can get to know yourself a little better:

Personality

You have a unique way of viewing the world. Your likes and dislikes, how you process information, whether you like to hide in the background or bask in the spotlight, whether you like to lead or you prefer to follow; on and on the list goes of the qualities that combine to create your unique personality. Some people are naturally filled with compassion. Others love to teach or solve problems. Some focus on what is right and wrong. Some like to encourage people. Some people are very relational, with others feeling most comfortable when serving others. Some are natural at business and very generous with their money.

There are many wonderful personality tests you can take to help you discover your own natural bent. I've included sources in the appendix in the back if you'd like to take one. If you've never taken a personality test before, I highly suggest you do so. The results can be very eye opening and not only help you understand how you're wired, but how people close to you are wired as well.

Gifts and Talents

You were born with a certain tool box at birth. Over time, some of these tools have become obvious to you: you may have an ear for music, be great with numbers, or be naturally coordinated. But even if you think you're all thumbs and dumber than a doorknob, trust me: you have gifts. You have talents. Maybe they are hard to see, but they're there.

While some gifts are obvious at a young age, others show up later. One of my friends was very shy when she was little and continued that way well into her adult years. But eventually she became a Brownie Troop leader, then created her own group for girls, and eventually became a public speaker. It took time for her leadership and speaking gifts to emerge and grow. The same is true for you. Who knows what seeds of greatness are sitting dormant in you right now? Maybe all it will take is a few splashes of hope and encouragement, and you'll find yourself doing more than you could have ever imagined.

Skills

A skill is what happens when we take a natural gift and develop it. Even if you have a gift for music or dance, you will have to practice for years to bring it to fulfillment. For some skills, the only gift you have to have is one of perseverance. Some skills can be achieved by anyone willing to take the time and effort to cultivate them.

There might be skills you have that you think are of little importance. But don't overlook them. Even "boring" talents, like organizational skills or being able to make a budget, can be a huge benefit in your destiny.

To summarize what we've said so far, the biggest barrier to your dream is you. A shift must occur in our mindset if we want to move forward into our destiny. We need to break the bad cycles of blame, fear, and a damaged self-identity to create positive change. Next, we'll talk about the spark that can move your destiny from park into overdrive.

8

THE AHA MOMENT

Hopefully by now, you're convinced that you have a destiny. Dreams are coming back to life and hope is rising. You are beginning to believe you are a person of great worth who can have an amazing life. You can see the unique qualities you possess and how that can translate into your personal calling. Even if some of these areas are still not clear to you, my goal is for you to be growing in hope as you read through these chapters.

Destiny is all about purpose, calling, and dreams in motion. So how do we get all these elements to connect and create forward momentum? What is needed is one thing: I call it the Aha Moment. This is the realization that you are not just seeing your desire and need for change, but that you are also ready to do something about it. The Aha Moment is all about triggering action, because action is required to get from where you are to where you want to be. Another way to say it is that you're sick and tired of being sick and tired, and you're ready to get off your backside and get going.

This Aha Moment doesn't have to be just for major changes in your life. It can a mini moment, like when you want to see improvement in one area of your life. Maybe you're finally going to organize your closet, lose those extra pounds, train for a marathon, quit smoking, or ask the boss for a raise. Whatever your goal may be, you need a moment of motivation, which becomes a turning point that translates into action.

The Aha Moment can come about in different ways. For some, it's a rock bottom experience. That was David's case when he was arrested for his D.U.I. That difficult time motivated him to make permanent changes he'd not been ready to make for years. Sometimes a crisis creates an Aha Moment, like it did for me when the loss of a high-paying job started me on my cake journey.

A major life event can spur the Aha Moment as well. Reaching a certain age, the birth of a child, getting married, the death of someone close to us, a graduation, or retirement can cause us to reflect on where we are and where we'd really like to be, and spur us into action. Sometimes seeing someone else taste the success we've always wanted helps us realize we can do it, too.

Make Your Own Moment

What if you haven't had a rock-bottom experience, a crisis, or other life event that has spurred you into action? Are you doomed to sit around and wait for one to happen to you? No, thankfully. Sometimes Aha Moments come looking for you, but that doesn't mean that you can't go looking for one of your own. Here's a few things to keep in mind to help your own "light bulb" click on and find the motivation you need to take action.

You need to understand the cost of not moving forward into your destiny and your dreams. What are you missing out on by not changing? What are the consequences of staying on your current course for the long term? What is the true gap between where you are and where you want to be? The answer to this question might be very sobering, but sometimes we need a misery factor or we'll just decide to stay comfortable where we are.

You also need to understand that you've given yourself permission to be where you are. I realize that sometimes life gives us situations we did not choose and did not want. But even in the midst of that, you get to decide whether you'll be a victim or a victor.

I'm going to turn on my momma mode here for just a minute, so don't tune me out. Just how long do you want to stay in your current situation? How long is long enough? Seriously, I will not apologize for wanting to get you out of your stuck condition. So let me ask you: How long before you decide to wake up? What will it take for you to stop looking back and start moving forward?

Only you can make that choice. I wanted David to change for me while he was battling his issues. But I had to realize that only he had the power to choose to change. The same is true for you. You can do it! The power to change is in you. You've got this! You are precious and your life has purpose. Don't sell yourself short.

Lies That Stand in Your Way

Your Aha Moment won't ever bear fruit if you believe any of the following lies:

"My dream is impossible. It's just too big and it's not practical."

Not true. Well, if your dream is to flap your arms and fly like a hummingbird, your dream might need a little revision. But I'm sure neighbors thought those Wright boys were delusional before they attached bicycle parts to some large wings and made aviation history. Your crazy dream might need some modification over time, but if you aim for **nothing**, you're sure to hit it.

"I'm just not capable of doing _____"

You are more capable than you think you are. Hard work and persistence don't take genius. Large tasks can be broken down into smaller, achievable steps. Skills can be developed. That's the lesson from my cake journey, when I worked super hard and researched and practiced until I could compete on national television. And guess what? I'm still learning. You don't have to be the best, but there is space for you. You can operate in your own brilliance.

"I don't have enough resources to start."

Then start with what you have. You'd laugh if you could see the workspace I use to create my custom cakes and the tools I started with. Nothing fancy at all. I guarantee that many of you reading this book have a larger and better equipped workspace than I do. But I didn't let my lack slow me down. I learned to max out what I had and today, I don't have the have the best of everything to accomplish my goals. Whenever I face a shortage, whether it's time, money, tools, space, the right people, etc., I find a way around it. It's not always easy, but it is possible.

"I just don't deserve it.
Someone like me can't have a fulfilling destiny."

Say what? Did those words actually come out of your mouth? I sure hope not, because if they did, I'd need to send you back a few pages and make you read some stuff again.

Seriously, I know that getting over a low self-esteem takes time and some folks are so beaten down it takes a while before they can truly see the amazing person they are. So hear me when I say to you that you not only deserve it, but the rest of us are waiting on you to step out, because our destiny can't come to pass without you.

Every day, I speak words of blessing over my children. I started with Valentino when he was in my womb and I've continued speaking over my children every day since. And I mean every day. I'm not exaggerating. I want to make sure they are built up with a strong, core identity, before the world and all its negativity takes its best shot at tearing them down. When the day comes that they face undeserved criticism, false comments and rude remarks, I want it to be second nature for them to brush those things aside and keep believing the truth about themselves.

Before they go to bed and after we say our prayers, I whisper in their ears the things I love about them, how it makes me feel, and how I appreciate and value them. I can see how they receive and respond to the affirmation in the way they react and behave with others.

My children couldn't affirm themselves when they were babies, so I sowed the truth of who they really are before they could talk. But now, if you ask them who they are, this is what they'll tell you:

I am the Head and Not the Tail
I am Above and Not Beneath.
I am Beautifully and Wonderfully Made.
I am Successful, I am Blessed, and Highly Favored.
I am fulfilling My Destiny.
I was created for Greatness.
I am a Voice in my Generation,
because I am a Child of God.

Perhaps no one has sown seeds of truth into your life. If no one is affirming you, then you must affirm yourself. You may not believe these words apply to you. And if your beliefs or faith is not the same as mine, you might choose different words to speak over yourself. But I promise you, if you say words of affirmation often enough, you will believe them. That change in your mindset will help you realize who you truly are and give you the courage to bring about the change that is needed in your situation.

My children only know these words to be truth. It is embedded in them. If you were to ask them who God says they are, they would repeat each affirmation by memory and most likely give you a "Hallelujah!" when they were finished. I can't imagine if I told them the complete opposite on a daily basis. Where would their confidence be then? Your words and the words of others can either build or destroy. We do reap what we sow.

The Pain/Change Factor

It's human nature to resist change. We all do it. Every year right after January 1, the gyms are packed with people exercising. By mid-March, the gyms are back to their normal clientele. Why is that? Because while we like the idea of change, we don't like the cost of change very much.

For true change to occur, we have to raise the pain factor of staying the same and lower the pain factor of change. In other words, we have reach the place where the pain of staying the same becomes higher than the cost of changing. For example, you'll willingly jump out of an upstairs window, if the house is on fire.

We've already discussed a part of the "pain" side, when I challenged you to realize the cost of staying where you are. Becoming miserable with your current situation will help push you out of your comfort zone and into the exciting unknown. Think about how you'd like to look back on your life when you reach the end of your journey. Do you want to be filled with regrets and wonder what could have been? If you're a parent, do you want to teach you kids to play it safe and settle for mediocrity? Take some time to seriously consider the downside of things remaining just as they are today. Is that what you really want in your future?

Let's work on lowering the "change" side of the equation. You need to realize that it doesn't take as much effort to change as you think. Even a journey of 1,000 miles begins with one step. You can baby step your way to your dreams. Reading this book is already a step in the right direction. It's just about moving forward, not figuring it all out or solving the entire problem before you move an inch. Just move forward.

Try choosing one simple step you can take each day toward your dreams. Sign up for that fitness class. Smoke one less cigarette. Make that appointment. Apply to one school. Put in one job application. Order a salad instead of fries.

Watch one tutorial. You get the idea. Start with something, anything, but start.

The key to having an effective Aha Moment is to start *now*. Don't wait. Even the process of moving forward in little ways is encouraging. It takes more energy to get something moving than it takes to keep it moving. So if you can go from 0 to 1 mile per hour, it will take even less energy to get to 2 miles an hour. And you'll start creating the positive momentum that will propel you into your destiny.

Your Aha Moment: Declare It!

Perhaps you're having an Aha Moment right now. All the things we've talked about might have sparked something within you and you've found the motivation you've been missing. If you're not quite at that point, that's fine as well. Either way, I'd like to pause and give you a chance to think over your own life and the destiny you'd like to have. Now is the time to take a step in the right direction.

There's something powerful about actually writing down and speaking out decisions we've made. This process seals them and makes them real and tangible. It causes us to solidify our resolve and create the action it takes for change to occur. Let me give you a few samples so you know what I mean.

First, here's one for a real minor issue many of us have. My day is so busy that I forget to drink enough water each day. My goal is 8 glasses of water, but I can go all day and not even drink one. But if I declare it, write it down, and make the water bottles available around the house, then my actual consumption of water changes immediately. So here's my Aha Moment declaration for increasing my water each day:

I declare that my body is precious and I want to live in health.

I will drink 8 glasses of water each day so I can be the best I can be.

Here's an example for a bigger issue. We'll pretend that you want to improve a key life relationship. Maybe it's with your spouse, a significant other, a child, or a parent. Just put his/her name in the blank:

I declare that _____ is important in my life. I choose to make _____ a priority and take daily steps to improve our relationship. I cannot control his/her actions, but I can control my own. I choose to love them, encourage them, forgive them, and put their needs about my own. Today I will make a point to_____

And you can fill in the last blank with an action point, such as thanking them for all the hard work they do, inviting them to dinner, offering them a back rub, or whatever is fitting in your situation. If you did this every day, can you see how, over time, your relationship would improve?

Now let's say someone is royally stuck. Their finances are a mess, their career is in shambles, and they just went through a painful divorce. That sounds like my situation, once upon a time. If I could go back to my younger self, this is the declaration I would make:

Elaine, you are precious. You are not a victim. You are capable, no matter how hard the road may seem. You got this, girl! Be the best that you can be in every season and every moment. If you act with intention and push your way through strategically, you will be able to see the open doors that are set in your path. You must be slow to speak and always listen, so you can receive words of wisdom as they come to help you on your journey. If you do your best, God will do the rest. Remember, your opportunity is always a handshake away. I believe in you!

If you have been stirred by what you've been reading and you're ready for change, I challenge you right now to take a moment, write down your own Aha Moment Declaration, and speak it out loud. Don't be shy. It's a small baby step to take, but a very crucial one. If you can't write it down, then it isn't real and chances are, in a few days' time, you'll forget what you decided altogether.

Do it now, if you can. There's no time like the present. It's only a better future that's at stake.

In Summary

In this chapter, we've discussed the Aha Moment — that light-bulb moment that creates the motivation to take action and move toward your destiny. Aha Moments can happen to us when we face a crisis, major life event, or see the success of others. If such a moment doesn't happen to us, we can help create our own by examining the cost of not changing, by overcoming the lies that hinder us, by affirming ourselves, and taking into account the pain/change factor. And finally, we discussed the importance of declaring our desire to change, looked at several examples, and encouraged you to make a declaration of your own.

Once your Aha Moment is made, you are ready for the next phase in your destiny journey. I'm going to show you the practical steps to translate your motivation into action.

9

MOVING IT FORWARD

Now that you've found the motivation to change, I'm going to show you some useful, straight-forward steps to put your desire to change into gear. Don't put these steps off, because our motivation can quickly fade if we don't take action. How you approach these steps will depend on the goal you've set. If it's something personal, say weight loss or reorganizing your home, your approach will be completely different from someone looking to change careers or start a new business. I've written the following steps to include many situations and it will be easy to customize your answers to fit your needs.

Clarify the Vision

There's an old phrase that says to write down the vision and make it plain. Whatever you see your destiny being, whatever your life purpose, calling and dreams are, write them down. Make them simple enough for a child to understand. Keep it short; there's no need to go into lots of detail at this point.

If nothing else, simply state what it is that you are trying to achieve.

You aren't limited to using words when clarifying your vision. Pictures are truly worth a thousand words and you might find that making a dream board or dream book works better for you. That's what I did when I started my cake journey. Once I moved beyond the basics, my desire for an actual location to showcase my edible art started to grow. I knew I wanted it to be spectacular, with a certain look that represented me, while allowing our potential guests to create memories and have a wonderful experience.

I took a binder and created sections for décor, menu, products, etc. Every time I saw or read something that would trigger an idea, I would take a picture of it, print it out, and place it in my binder. I was doing Pinterest before there was a Pinterest. If I ever feel like my dream is taking too long to come true, I can just open my dream book and dream of what will be. My dreams may look like a simple scrapbook to other people, but nothing inside is scrap to me. One day, when my dream of a brick and mortar location becomes a reality, I'll proudly display my dream book so I can inspire the dreams of others.

"But what if my dream doesn't come true? What then?" you may ask. Good question. Let's use my dream book as an example. What if, in spite of all my efforts, my dream of an Enticing Cake Boutique location never comes to pass? Will it have all been in vain? No. Not at all. My dream book has kept fueling my passion. It has caused me to reach smaller dreams on the way to my "big" one. Even if the big dream you have today does not come true, the mere attempt of it will bring many blessings you'd never have if you never try.

What Are Your Positives?

Next, take an assessment of your positives. This will include both intangible things, like attitudes, benefits, and opportunities, as well as tangible things, like tools or money. If you've ever watched one of those outdoor survival shows, one of the first things they always do is take an assessment of their current situation. For example, they might list that no one is hurt, they have three hours before sundown, and that the forest up ahead will provide them with shelter. Next, they take an inventory of everything they have at their disposal, no matter how insignificant it may seem. A half-used lip balm, pieces of dental floss, shoe strings, and an old battery are later transformed into a candle, a trap for catching their next meal, and a fire source. By properly evaluating their positives, they can survive and thrive.

You don't have to go through your cabinets and desk drawers and list every paper clip, but when you start looking at what you actually have and what you have access to, the list will be longer than you expect. Here are a few positives to consider:

- What are the benefits of this goal?
- What personality traits do you have that will benefit

you in this endeavor?

- What opportunities are there that you can take advantage of?
- Who are the people in your life that you know, either personally or professionally, that can help you?
- What organizations are in your area (Chamber of Commerce, service groups, non-profits, etc.) that you can utilize for information or assistance?
- What skills and talents do you have? (List them all, even if you think they don't apply to your goal.)
- What education and/or licenses do you currently hold? Could some licenses be reactivated if need be?
- How much money do you have access to, including liquid, non-liquid, and credit?
- What other hard assets do you have or have access to, such as equipment, space, and storage?
- How much time can you set aside for this goal?

When I started my cake journey, the benefits of my goal were that I would gain a way to help financially support my family in a way that would fulfill me. I had art skills and because I had no job, I had time. I could take classes at Michaels and use their coupons to get the tools I needed with my limited income. I had the personality trait of an optimist and a go-getter, which helped me learn quickly and kept me focused. I didn't know anyone in the cake business to start, but I soon developed strategic relationships along the way. The Chamber of Commerce was very helpful with free advice on starting my business.

You might be surprised when you take an inventory of all your resources. You might view things in a different light when you start to focus on the solution instead of the problem. But we do have to be realists and we can't ignore the obvious, which brings us to the next step:

What Are Your Negatives?

You also need to take an assessment of the barriers you'll have to overcome or work around to reach you dreams. Mind you, these aren't dream-killers, but they will stop your dreams cold if you don't deal with them.

Don't let this list discourage you. See it as an important step to help you reach your goal. Be honest with yourself and your situation. Whatever the negative, you'll be able to find a way to handle it. Here's a list of negatives to consider:

- What is the downside of going for this dream?
- What personality traits will you need to overcome in order to be successful?
- Are there relationships in your life that might make going for this dream difficult?
- What weaknesses do you have in your current skill set that you will need to compensate for?
- Where does your education fall short?
- How much money do you need to reach the next level?
- What hard assets do you lack, such as tools, equipment, space, storage, etc.?

- What time constraints will you need to work around to accomplish your goal?
- What will you have to say "no" to in order to say "yes" to this dream?

Sometimes we must let go of the good thing in order to grab hold of the best thing. Letting go of something that is good can be painful. Saying yes in one area means we need to say many no's in others. Better to face up to this fact and come up with a strategy to handle it rather than be blindsided down the road and end up in a ditch.

Some negatives can be turned into positives. The fact that you don't have much money might make you eligible for scholarships or grants. Maybe you don't have a certain skill but you can find a way to barter with someone who does and needs yours in return. The fact that you don't own a large company might mean you can stay lean, mean, and nimble, and can quickly respond to changes in the marketplace.

If you have personality traits you need to compensate for, like being a procrastinator, or if like me, you can be a bit forgetful, you can easily find ways to keep yourself accountable or utilize a reminder system. I want to encourage you that your negatives don't have to keep you from your dreams.

Make a Plan

Now that you have a made your goal clear, and you've listed all your positives as well as your negatives, it's time to make a plan of action to utilize your resources and overcome your barriers. Even if a clear path to the end goal isn't completely clear, the first initial steps should be obvious enough. Your plan can keep developing and evolving, but the important thing is to actually start.

Be practical. Don't bite off more than you can chew. You'll only get discouraged when you haven't met your unrealistic goals. Keep it simple. If you can't easily explain your plan to someone else, then it is too complicated.

Asking for advice from someone else who's been there and done that is an excellent idea. Whether it's weight loss, going back to school, or bringing a new invention to market, the advice of someone who is ahead of you in the journey is priceless.

Each day, do something to move forward, even if it is small. We talked about baby steps before and that's what it can feel like. But those baby steps add up over time. They really do. Sometimes you can move forward quickly toward your dream and other times it's slow going. The important thing is to keep moving forward.

Sometimes it can even seem like you're going backwards, but that can be just a transition time in your journey. One time, I was renting a commercial kitchen with someone else and the situation changed so that I no longer had the demand to justify renting the space. But it wasn't a defeat, just a temporary adjustment.

In the same way it's important to write down your vision, you need to write down your plan. Even if you only write down the biggest points, put pen to paper or keep track of your strategy electronically. Include short term, midterm, and long term goals. If you have a very specific objective in mind, backward planning is a great way to figure out how and when you need to get from here to there.

Keep the Ball Rolling

Congratulations! You're on your way. You've found motivation to move forward, clearly defined and written down your vision, you've taken personal inventory of your situation and made a plan of action. And you've taken your first baby steps to your dreams. (If you haven't actually done these things, that's OK. You have my permission to keep reading. But I hope that at some point, you will take these important, life-changing steps.)

With these steps behind you, you're no longer stuck on the road of your destiny. Now that you've got the ball rolling, you want to keep it going. And believe me, there will be plenty of opportunities for your forward momentum to come to a screeching halt. You had to take steps to get unstuck. You must take steps to stay unstuck.

The most important step you can do to keep the ball rolling is to take the vision you wrote down earlier and put it where you will see it often. Write it on a post-it note and stick it on your bathroom mirror or near your computer screen.

Put a note on the dash of your car or on your refrigerator. If you keep your vision in front of you, it will grow inside of you.

Another dream accelerator is to surround yourself with people who will support you and your dream. Baby dreams need nurturing. They don't do well in harsh environments. If you have to live under the blistering heat of constant critical comments and ridicule, you'll need to find a way to set up some healthy boundaries and get out of that toxic situation.

Find people who will feed your dream, people who will build you up and encourage you on your way. Find people who are already living the dream you want and spend time with them. By hanging around successful people, you'll pick up on their successful ways.

If you want to get fit and lose weight, but you spend all your free time with couch potatoes, chances are slim that you ever will be. If you're starting a business, find ways to spend time with successful small business owners. You get the idea. That isn't to say that you cut off your old relationships, but if you are moving forward into new territory, you'll want to establish new healthy relationships to go with it.

Give Yourself Permission

The path forward will not be a perfectly straight line. There will be some ups and downs along the way, and if you can anticipate that in advance, you'll be prepared when those dips happen. Here are areas where you need to give yourself permission:

Give yourself permission to fail. Very few people knock it out of the park their first time at bat. Some of the most successful business people have gone bankrupt at least once. Even Edison took 1,000 tries before he unlocked the secret to the light bulb. Tripping and falling isn't true failure — giving up and not trying again is. Realize now that not every decision will end the way you plan. This brings us to the next related permission:

Give yourself permission to not be perfect. Being imperfect is far short of failing, but making mistakes, even small ones, can be painful. If you are a perfectionist, this is one area where you will need to extend yourself some grace, and often. No one is perfect and that's a fact. I'm so glad that our destiny does not depend on our ability to be faultless.

I wish you could see a sugar artist put a cake together. You would be surprised at how many little mistakes are made along the way. Fondant cracks are covered with roses, unlevel cakes are visually repaired with extra frosting, and fancy bag work at the bottom can hide an unclean edge. In life, as with cakes, it's impossible to avoid mistakes. The trick is to know how to handle a mistake when it happens. Don't beat yourself up. Just deal with it, learn from it, put it behind you, and keep moving forward.

<u>Give yourself permission to be frustrated.</u> All sorts of things can frustrate us. Sometimes we get tired of waiting for our dreams to come true. I call it a dream temper tantrum, and I've had my share of those: all those times that I didn't make the *Next Great Baker*, when a potential client chose someone else instead of me to make their cake, or when I thought the *Cake Adore* book had passed me by. Being frustrated means that you are passionate and driven, and that's a good thing. Give yourself permission to be impatient and realize that good things come to those who wait.

<u>Give yourself permission to be discouraged.</u> It's not all sunshine and roses on the path of your destiny. There will be some cloudy days ahead. If you keep encouraging yourself with daily affirmations, those days of discouragement won't derail your dreams. Some days will be scary, so give yourself permission to be afraid. Courage isn't the lack of fear, but moving forward even when you are afraid.

<u>Give yourself permission to cry.</u> If you're the kind of person I am, this is a given. But you've got to let your emotions out once in a while so you can take a deep breath and regroup. Holding all those intense feelings inside won't do you or your loved ones any good.

<u>Give yourself permission to be affirmed and encouraged.</u> This one is so important to me, I have a dream to write a book on this subject someday. I've already shared with you the affirmations I've spoken over my children every day of their lives. We can speak death or we can speak life over

ourselves. It's easy to speak negative words, but we must be very purposeful in speaking positive ones. Some of you may have been a doormat for so long that you need extra reinforcement.

There are many other areas that you need to give yourself permission in the positive. Give yourself permission to be daring. Don't be afraid to take a risk and go for the stars. Give yourself permission to grow. Step out of your comfort zone and stretch into your possibility. Give yourself permission to believe: believe in your dream, yourself, and believe in others.

Here's one that's very important: <u>give yourself permission to rest, recharge, and have your needs met</u>. You can't give what you don't have. You can't pour out of an empty cup. Mothers especially tend to put their own needs in last place and think they are being selfish if they do something for themselves. It is not selfish to make sure you are healthy and whole.

Sometimes your dream path needs adjustments, so <u>give yourself permission to change course.</u> Don't see it as a failure if your plans don't succeed and you have to take a different path. It's just a part of your journey.

Don't worry about being liked by everyone else. <u>Give yourself permission to be different, to be original</u>. That also means you'll need to give yourself permission to not fit in and be misunderstood. It can be hard to go against the flow and not meet the expectations of others, but why let their limited mindset hold you back?

You are wired for connection and your destiny isn't just about you, so be inclusive. Don't cut people out because of their background, personality, or quirks. If you give them a chance, you might discover they have hidden gifts that will be a blessing to you.

Two important lessons my Grandpa Oscar taught me were to be fair and to be generous. He taught me to always do the right thing and to make sure I could sleep at night with a clear conscience. Grandpa modelled generosity every day of his life. He taught me to be giving now, not to wait until I was rich.

He said, "If you don't give now, you won't give when you're rich."

And we need to give more than our money. We need to be generous with our time, love, encouragement, wisdom and advice, meals, physical help, etc. Every time we are generous, we are building connection with others and sowing seeds that will reap us blessings in the future.

The writing of this book is one example of this important sowing and reaping principle. As my friend, Julie, shared in the book's foreword, I sowed into her life at a vulnerable time, not knowing that later she would be the one to help me write this book. I never dreamed that the payback would be so great. But that's the principle we release when we are generous toward others. The harvest may not come from the same place where we sowed the seed, but the harvest will come.

One last principle I'd like to share is another one from Grandpa Oscar. He taught me to treat people with dignity and to not manipulate others to get what I want. We shouldn't take unfair advantage of another's weakness. We don't have to tear others down to get ahead. That's another kind of sowing and reaping, and if you sow seeds of manipulation, unfairness, and greed, you'll reap a harvest from that too, but not the kind of harvest you hoped for.

In Summary

In this chapter, we discussed important action points you can take to move forward once you've had your Aha Moment: clarify your vision, take an assessment of your positives and negatives, make a plan of action, and act on it. Once you're in motion, we shared how to keep the ball rolling by reminding yourself often of your goals, surrounding yourself with encouraging people and environments, giving yourself permission along the way to be prepared for different road bumps, and to make choices that will feed your fire.

But how do you know when you've achieved success? How do you know when you've arrived and your life is finally one of fulfillment?

10

REDEFINING SUCCESS

We've covered a lot of ground in a short time. I've shared many practical tips about destiny, overcoming the barrier to your dreams, how to find motivation, and how to keep the ball rolling. But in this chapter, I want to do something a little different and share my philosophy of success.

In our culture, we are bombarded by messages about success. Celebrities flaunt it, advertisements push it, and salespeople promise it. The world seems to define success as the accumulation of wealth, fame, and accolades. Very few of us will ever make the Forbes 500 list, walk the red carpet, or get one million likes on Twitter. With the definition of success set so high, how can we ever hope to attain it?

We can't. It just isn't possible. At least, we can't attain that definition of success. But that is not what true success is. You only need to look just below the surface of those so-called "successful people" to see that the world's definition is simply a lie. Some of the most miserable people in the world are the ones we envy the most. So why do we use them as our standard?

Let's set a new standard of success instead. What if we redefined success in a way that anyone can achieve? Not to lower the bar, but to create a definition that has real meaning and real purpose—something far more significant than just reaching the top of the heap. Let me share with you my definition of success.

What Success is Not

First, let me tell you what it's not. It's not a destination. It's not arriving. You never "arrive." That's just a myth people chase. I found that out firsthand when David and I were chosen as contestants on the *Next Great Baker*. I had been pursuing that hard-to-achieve dream for several years, but once my dream finally came true, I realized that it was only a stepping stone to the next level. I didn't "arrive" when I put on that red chef coat. It was just a milepost along my path.

Success is not gaining a certain level of wealth or material possessions. When do you ever have enough? Does having $10,000 in savings make you successful? What about $100,000 or $100,000,000? If that is our definition of success, then what about all the billions of people in the world living in places where they will never have the opportunity to earn that much? Are they doomed to never taste success? I think not.

Success is not about being highly respected or well known in society. We can all think of examples of people who were once widely admired, yet experienced great falls from grace when secret skeletons they'd been hiding in their closets came to light.

Success can't be bought and it can't be sold. You can't steal someone else's if you don't have your own. You can't borrow someone else's success, even if they want to give it to you.

Success isn't all about you and getting everything you want. It certainly isn't defined by having a life without problems, challenges, disappointments, or struggles. No one would ever be successful if that were the case.

What Success Is

To me, this is what success is: It's a forward-thinking perspective that is pursuing your destiny, with your unique life purpose, calling, and dreams. Success is appreciating the blessings you have right now while, at the same time, looking forward to a brighter tomorrow.

Success says, "I can" instead of "I can't." It looks for a solution instead of complaining about the problem. Success speaks life and not death. Success, when it stumbles, gets back up and tries again.

Success is a giver, not a taker. Success knows when to hang on, and when to let go. Success isn't about showing off, but about giving back. It's a state of mind and a way of living. Success isn't about having a fancy lifestyle, but it's the way you do life.

Success isn't about trying to be a copy of everyone else, but it's about being comfortable in your own skin. It's not about who you know; it's about knowing who you are. Success is not about envying others, but rejoicing with them in their victories. Success isn't about competing against others, but finding ways to complement them.

To go back to the words of affirmation I speak over my children, success is knowing that you are the head and not the tail, that you are above and not beneath. It's walking out the truth that you are wonderful and amazing, and that because you are a person of value, you can value others.

Success is knowing that you have a voice in your generation because you were created with greatness in mind. Walking out your destiny, whatever that may be, means you are walking in success.

Based on my definition of success, you can start walking in success today, even if your external situation doesn't change right away. That's because success is more about how you think and your perspective than it is about your material situation. When you have the right mindset, success is the natural by-product. You simply can't have success without it.

The source of your success doesn't come from outside of you, but from within. My Grandpa Oscar was the perfect example of this. On the outside, he looked like he needed a handout or a hand up, wearing his holey shirt, a pair of paint-spattered boating moccasins, and driving around in his old hoopty car. But he had a heart of gold and everyone around him knew it. That's because his greatness came from who he was. His greatness created his wealth, not the other way around.

That's how true success works. Once you know who you are, your success goes with you. If you go through a rough spot, it doesn't mean you're a failure. The seeds of greatness you carry will bear fruit in the end if you don't give up.

Successful people do share some common traits. For one, they stay active and intentional in pursuing their destiny. Their goals are focused and clearly defined. They understand that success is ongoing, without a ceiling to limit it. While they enjoy their lives, they aren't satisfied unless they are growing and continuing to develop in every area. They know they can keep learning, expanding, and stretching the boundaries of what they once thought was possible.

Successful people are determined to create a legacy to pass on to others. They want to nurture and bless and help others on their journey. They know that success breeds success, not just for themselves, but also for others. Successful people have found the secret to being content with themselves and in whatever situation they face, while at the same time reaching out for more.

Defining Success for Yourself

When it comes to success, you need to define what it means to you. Because we have different dreams, one person might find success while teaching in a public school and being connected to their community, while another person finds success running an international multi-million-dollar corporation. We can't say that the multi-millionaire is more successful than the public-school teacher. Some of the most miserable people in the world have big bank accounts. Again, money alone can't be a measure of success. Both people can be equally successful.

There are different levels of success as well. You can feel complete after reaching a certain goal, but you might desire to move on to the next level. Give yourself permission to want more. If you start a successful bakery, maybe you'll want to add a location. Who knows? Maybe you'll want to start a franchise.

You also need to give yourself permission to be content. Having children is a great example. Some are happy to stop with one. Others don't feel complete unless they have a houseful. I have two kids while my co-writer, Julie, has seven. We're both content with what we have and can't imagine it any other way.

Not everyone wants to have a huge business. Not everyone who goes to the gym wants to be a professional body builder. The beauty of success is that you can have it at all levels. Each level will require a different strategy, but whichever level you choose to operate on is entirely up to you.

I encourage you to take a moment and define success for yourself. It's how you want to approach your destiny and dreams, combined with the intangibles that make you feel complete and fulfilled. As you do so, don't forget to keep in mind the blessings you have in your hand right now. Some blessings, like family and friends, are priceless. So is being content with ourselves.

My personal definition of success is to live a full, healthy, long life, while enjoying great experiences and wonderful memories with the people that I love the most. I want to be actively inspiring and providing opportunities for people to succeed. I desire to be financially free; I want to control my finances and not have my finances controlling me. Success to me is seeing the development in my children's character because of the affirming investments I poured into them.

Our journey together is almost over. I've so enjoyed sharing my life journey with you and the message of how to turn your disappointment into destiny. I have just a few more secrets up my sleeve and some dreams to share, so don't skip the final chapter.

11

NOT THE END,
JUST THE BEGINNING

From the tiny state of Delaware, through the gritty streets of Philly, past the island of Puerto Rico, to the state of Florida and onto an international television show, we certainly have covered a lot of territory. And that's without considering all the ups and downs of my crazy life. I could have never made it without my faith, my family, and my friends.

After I shared my personal journey, I showed you the truths I've learned behind the scenes. We covered so many topics in a short space, but I wanted to give you as many tools as I could to help you on your journey. And I didn't write this just for you; I also wrote it for myself. I wish you could see my personal copy of this book, because I've taken notes and used highlighters all over the place. This book is a valuable resource I plan to keep around, not because I wrote it, but because I need it.

I have just a few loose ends to tie up from the story of my life. One of my greatest joys was that before he passed away, my beloved Grandpa Oscar was able to watch David and I as we competed on TLC's *Next Great Baker*. He was so proud of us, and very interested in the show and our experience there. I know even now he is smiling down on me, and I will be eternally grateful for his positive influence in my life.

If you wondered what happened to the cousin that moved in with me during my "starving season," I am happy to say that she is doing very well and today works as a youth pastor. While the path to her fulfilled life has had its own twists and turns, she has persevered to become a remarkable young woman. Her greatest compliment to me was after the passing of our grandfather, when she told me I had become her Grandpa Oscar.

What's Next for Me

As I close this chapter of my life, a new one is already unfolding. I'm setting new dreams as other dreams are coming true. Since I spoke at the Miami Culinary Institute's Chef Coat ceremony, my cake business has continued to grow. With my newly expanded website, I'm moving into video tutorials and sharing the secrets of my favorite decorating tools and our recipe book. We are launching a whole line of Enticing Edibles that will melt in your mouth and expanding our retail apparel line to add to the signature aprons we already have available.

After the wonderful experience of being on TLC's *Next Great Baker*, I was honored to be chosen by the Food Network to appear on *Cake Wars Season 3* in July, 2016. I was excited about another opportunity to do what I love best on national television, but I wanted to make sure my heart was in the right place.

As I was flying out for the taping of the show, I said to myself, "Elaine, do your best and God will do the rest. The outcome doesn't matter; the point is that you went for it, and that you keep setting the bar higher and higher."

I knew I had two little ones at home that were watching my every move. They see the way I work, the way I speak, how I handle situations, and how I act and react. I wanted them to see that this is just the beginning for this amazing journey I call life. I only have one life to live and I want to live it to the fullest.

My partner on the show was Bethany Davis of Betnie Bakes, a fellow competitor from *Next Great Baker* and an excellent sculptor. Our theme was Disney's *Beauty and the Beast* and while we didn't win, we were proud of our strong second place finish and our amazing cake. But I was even more proud that I stepped out, took a risk, and pushed myself to reach even higher than before.

Later in the summer of 2016, I had the honoring of hosting the chef stage at Orlando's Latin Food and Wine Festival. Representing my own culture at such a prestigious event reminded me that there is so much more in store for this Latina and that the sky is the limit.

I hope you enjoyed reading my first book, because I have more book ideas waiting to be developed. I also dream of travelling the world, speaking hope to those who feel stuck and encouraging those who want to change and make a difference.

I still have my eyes out for my first brick and mortar shop. I hope that one day, my Enticing Cake Boutique will be known as a business that not only serves the community with great memories and mouthwatering desserts, but a place where we can offer employment opportunities so that others can get a fresh start at building their future dreams.

What's Next for You?

This chapter and this book has come to end, but for both of us, this is just the beginning. Are you ready to be next? Are you motivated to take the first step toward your exciting destiny? Are you prepared to face your disappointments head on, deal with them, and turn them into the life you've always wanted?

If so, then I've accomplished my goal. The reason this book was written in the first place was because of my passion to see people set free and released into the fulfilled life they were created to live. I believe in you!

My wish for you is that somewhere deep inside, you find that flicker of light that's just waiting to become a full-blown fire. I hope you can discover your gifts, your talents, and your fullest potential, so in your dark season, you can find the light at the end of the tunnel. I want you to affirm and empower yourself to learn something new and to make a difference in your life and in those around you. And I wish for you to be the better version of you; the one you were intended to be.

The truths I've shared with you in this book are the very principles that had to be walked out to actually create the book. Believe me, it takes courage to step out in boldness and put your name on the cover of something so personal and so revealing. It takes guts to gather all the thoughts that you're so passionate about and share them with the world. There were roadblocks and speed bumps along the way, but each one was overcome and you hold the result of all that blood, sweat, and tears in your hands.

Your destiny is now in your hands. I've shown you the path to achieve it, but only you can make the choice to fulfill it. Will you make that choice? It's only your future that's at stake. Don't wait. Don't hesitate, because you're next! It's time to turn your disappointment into destiny.

Appendix

Here's a list of additional books and resources for those who want to go deeper into their destiny journey:

Books:

Stepping into Greatness, by Dr. Mark Chironna; Charisma Media.
Release Your Brilliance, by Simon T. Bailey; Harper Collins.
The Power of Positive Thinking, by Norman Vincent Peale; Touchstone.
How to Fulfill Your Divine Destiny, by Kenneth Hagin, Jr.; Faith Library Publications.
Boundaries, by Dr. Henry Cloud and Dr. John Townsend; Zondervan.
Seven Desires of Every Heart, by Debra Lasser and Mark R. Lasser; Zondervan.

Personality Tests:

Myers-Briggs Assessment: www.mbtionline.com
DISC, *Uniquely You:* uniquelyyou.org

About the Authors:

Known as "La Chica Dulce" (The Sweet Girl), **Elaine Duran** has been recognized as one of the baking industry's leading cake designers. With appearances on TLC's *Next Great Baker*, and Food Network's *Cake Wars*, Elaine has worked alongside renowned baking and cake professionals including Buddy Valastro, Jacques Torres, and Ron Ben Israel. Elaine's sugar artistry has been featured in numerous magazines and media outlets, including *Cake Central Magazine*, *The Daily Buzz*, and *Telemundo Orlando*, to name a few. Founded in 2010, her Enticing Cake Boutique is one of Central Florida's premier custom cake bakeries, specializing in stunning wedding cakes and 3D celebration cakes. Elaine lives with her beloved husband, David, and their two children in Kissimmee, Florida. Learn more at www.enticingcakeboutique.com. To connect with Elaine, follow her on Facebook at Elaine Duran.

Julie Voudrie began her writing career in the '90s when she and her husband owned their own publishing company, creating audio dramas, books, and an internationally-aired radio program for children. In 2014, Julie, along with her daughter, Danielle, appeared on TLC's *Next Great Baker Season 4* as the Pink Team and won the Hometown Dessert Challenge. Julie is a regularly featured chef on WJHL-TV's *Daytime Tri-Cities,* and teaches baking classes at East Tennessee State University. But baking is but one of Julie's many talents. She's also a singer, songwriter, author, and public speaker who pulls from her many life experiences – adoptive mother, homeschooler, former missionary, and entrepreneur – to create powerful messages that touch hearts and lives. Julie currently lives in Gray, Tennessee with Jeff, her husband of 30 years, and six of her seven children. Learn more at www.bakingwithjulie.com. To connect with Julie, follow her on all social media at Baking with Julie or email at julie@bakingwithjulie.com.

39688125R00099

Made in the USA
Middletown, DE
23 January 2017